# PUPPETS of POLITICAL PROPAGANDA

*Time to pull our own strings!*

Dr. Bob O'Connor

Total Health Publications
2020

# TABLE OF CONTENTS

The title, "Puppets of Political Propaganda" is designed to emphasize how we are all puppets dancing from the strings of the capitalists and their captive legislators and administrators. But may I say here, that not all legislators are ensnared in the web of the industrialists. Thank God-- or their parents, or their teachers, or their values-- for that! We are inundated with propaganda and promises by capitalists, and their advertising agencies, and by our politicians, and their varied use of social media and commercial advertising. Facts, faith, and fake news whirl through our environments influencing our opinions and directing our behavior.

## PRIVATE AND GOVERNMENTAL PROPAGANDA

Propaganda is from a Latin word meaning "to spread." Its modern use can be traced to a Catholic organization formed 400 years ago, "The Organization for the Propagation of the Faith." We can be influenced by both positive or negative messages.

NEGATIVE

➢ "Be born again or you will go to hell."

➢ "Wear your seat belt or you will be seriously injured or killed if you are in an accident."

➢ "Wash your hands or you may acquire the virus."

POSITIVE

➢ "Corona virus isn't a big worry"

➢ "It's for the American people."

➢ "Elect me and I'll eliminate the national debt in eight years."

Mitch McConnell tells us that the tax bill was "for the good of the American people," even though the major beneficiaries were the super-rich and the corporations, and even though the borrowing to pay for the bill increased our national debt by a trillion dollars and cost every American—man, woman and child--$3030 plus the yearly interest on that amount.

Donald Trump made his first statement regarding the corona virus on January 22, 2020 after the first American was diagnosed. He said, "We have no problem with the virus. And we have it totally under control. It's one person coming in from China, and we have it under control. It's going to be just fine." By this point, the seriousness of the virus was becoming clearer. It had spread from China to four other countries. China was starting to take drastic measures and was on the verge of closing off the city of Wuhan. As of this writing (April 7, 2020), the American death toll is 11,300 of the 360,000 existing cases.

On March 12, 2020 with 1323 confirmed cases, he said he had a "hunch that the death-rate will be under 1% of cases." The official estimate was 3.4%. In two weeks, the number of cases exceeded 100,000 and 1700 deaths, for a 1.7% death-rate. The next day it was a 1.8% death-rate. Now it is 3%.

The death-rate was rising because the active cases will either be cured or die. Those that die will raise the present death-rate. By late March the U.S. had more cases than any other country, even China— and China has three times the population that America has. In Italy, about 10% of people known to be infected have died—including 9,000 patients and more than 50 doctors. In Iran and Spain, the case fatality rate is higher than 7%. But in South Korea and it's less than 2%. And in Germany, the figure is close to 0.5%. The CDC tells us that the number of American deaths is underestimated because all who have died have not been tested for the virus. Their deaths may be listed only as pneumonia, when COVID-19 was the cause of the illness.

Trump's propaganda continued. "We inherited a broken test," Trump said on March 30 on Fox News. But there was no test.

Later in the day, he complained that his administration wasn't getting enough credit for overcoming what he claimed was a "broken testing system" in order to get a coronavirus test up and running. He then reiterated that the U.S. implemented a travel ban "way ahead of anybody else." This is false. China, and Italy were among the countries that had long-since enacted travel bans.

He could have insisted that the United States ramp up efforts to produce test kits. He could have emphasized the risks that the virus presented and urged Americans to take precautions if they had reason to believe they were sick. He could have released the protective equipment and ventilators in the Federal stockpile to the states earlier instead of insisting that they were only for Federal emergencies. The law that President Clinton signed was for whichever jurisdiction needed it—states, municipalities and territories. Both Bush and Obama had used it for states.

He could have used the powers of the presidency to reduce the number of people who would ultimately get sick. OR, he could continue to minimize the illness and death realities and focus on the economy. His $5 trillion addition to the national debt cost every American $15,150, plus interest, so far. If it resulted in your leaving the ranks of the unemployed, it is probably worth it. If you are a stock trading capitalist, it was worth it—at least until mid-February of 2020 when the stock market tanked. If you are in the top 10% in wealth, it was worth it. Unfortunately, the majority of people in the nation are not in these three categories.

Norway gave more to individuals than did the U.S. in attempting to heal the economic harm of COVID-19, but it took the billions from its savings, rather than borrowing! But then, the U.S. has no savings and Norway has its Oil Fund!

## CAPITALIST PROPAGANDA

But capitalists do their share of propagandizing. You remember the Boeing 737 MAX crashes due to their mis-engineering a computer program. The CEO attempted to blame the pilots. Yet, it was widely reported that Boeing didn't notify its 737 MAX customers that it had deactivated a safety feature that was designed to warn pilots that the angle-of-attack sensors were malfunctioning. According to a statement by Southwest Airlines, this safety feature was "depicted to us by Boeing as operable on all MAX aircraft." In reality, this was apparently not the case.

Advertising propaganda is similarly sending a positive message

- Harley Davidson – American by Birth. Rebel by Choice.
- Porsche – There is no substitute.
- Walmart – Save Money. Live Better.
- Nike – Just do it.
- Calvin Klein – Between love and madness lies obsession.
- Levis – Quality never goes out of style.
- PlayStation – Live in your world. Play in ours.

## IS PRIVATE BETTER THAN PUBLIC?

The capitalist propaganda says, YES. In some areas, private enterprise, the capitalists, do a better job than the state, but in many areas, the state does a better job, and does it cheaper. Although, the propaganda of the capitalists would have us believe otherwise! In the last few years we have seen Bernie Sanders and Elizabeth Warren propose programs that offer more welfare programs to the populace, like free university education and universal health care. Elizabeth seeks higher taxes on the rich to pay for it. Bernie wants more socialism---more government ownership of some businesses. But neither of these are "The American Way," as we have been repeatedly told.

And how have we learned the "American Way?" We have learned through decades of propaganda. The message has become so pervasive that most citizens from the President to the homeless are likely to believe it. Our legislators believe it! Our judges believe it! In fact, the Supreme Court ruled that a corporation is a "person" and as such is entitled to give as much as it wants to any elections. This was certain to increase their lobbying efforts and ensure that the legislators and executives will continue to propel the propaganda. After all, money talks, and it speaks loud and long. Ah! the American way!

Capitalists, through their corporations, can now give as much money to its candidates as it likes. In 2010, in Citizens United v. The Federal Election Commission (558 U.S. 310) the Court decided that corporations were people and that they can give to election campaigns. Then, in 2014 in McCutcheon v. Federal Election Commission (572 U.S. 185) it was decided that there was no limit to the contributions. This was another 5-4 decision.

These decisions overturned a number of previous Supreme Court cases and laws that began to be enacted from the time of Watergate and culminated in the McCain-Feingold and Shay-Meehan bills which, in combination, were signed by George W. Bush. The legislative bills were bipartisan, with about 25% of Republicans and 90% of Democrats voting for them. But the Supreme Court decided that not only are corporations people, but they are entitled to First Amendment free-speech rights and that the legislature cannot take those rights away from the corporations, or should we say, the capitalists.

Justice John Paul Stevens, commenting on a related case, McConnell v Federal Election Commission, believed that corporations have become too powerful in the electoral system, when he said that it is "a rejection of the common sense of the American people, who have recognized and need to prevent corporations from undermining self-government."

Lawyers are adept at changing meanings or inventing meanings to further their interests, or the interests of their clients. Since humans first stumbled out of their caves, they saw others as being people, like them. Throughout history we have agreed that humans are the only people. Dogs aren't people. Monkeys aren't people. Even chimpanzees are not people. Then why are corporations suddenly defined as people? They are not citizens, but often they have been born in America. What about a corporation that was born in Germany, like Volkswagen. Is it now an American person or citizen?

In an article in The Atlantic, by Adam Winkler, a law professor at UCLA, it concludes that "personhood" was erroneously conferred on corporations when Leland Stanford's Southern Pacific Railroad Company was being taxed for property it owned when people are not then taxed on their property. His lawyers used the 14th Amendment, which was enacted to protect the rights of freed slaves, to suddenly protect corporate interests.

Stanford's lawyer, Roscoe Conkling, had been a member of Congress that had drafted the 14th Amendment. He was the last committee member still alive. He said that the committee meant to include corporations under "persons" in the amendment.

He offered a journal as proof of what said. But years later, the journal was read by historians and found no evidence of corporations being included as "persons" in that Constitutional amendment. The rights of corporations were not ever raised in the debates, as far as we can tell.

So here we have a lie which was used to prove legislative intent for the 14th Amendment. The Supreme Court often refuses to admit the Preamble to the Constitution, which is very clear, as the legislative intent relative to its provisions-- particularly to the Bill of Rights. Judges may, or may not, look for legislative intent to bolster their arguments—depending on their prejudices.

A few years later, Justice Stephen J Field, a pro corporation justice, and friend of Leland Stanford, had advised Stanford on which lawyers to hire for his cases. He therefore should have recused himself from the case. Of course, he did not. Meanwhile the official reporter of Supreme Court decisions, J.C. Bancroft Davis, a former railroad president, cited the earlier Supreme Court decision, involving Southern Pacific Railroad, which did not rule that corporations were persons, and stated that the decision had found that they were, in fact, persons according to the 14th Amendment

If you would like to read the whole article, here is the link.

https://www.theatlantic.com/business/archive/2018/03/corporations-people-adam-winkler/554852/

FINANCING THE GOVERNMENT

Governments need a certain amount of money to handle general operating expenses, military preparedness, any welfare programs, and for emergencies—like the corona virus pandemic.

This income has to come from:
> Immediate taxes (individual and corporate—income and use taxes),
> Delayed taxation by borrowing or devaluing currency,
> Government ownership of some of the means of production (socialism).

Most countries use all three to some degree. The U.S. prefers to emphasize the first two.

The Nordic countries (Finland plus the Scandinavian countries of Norway, Sweden, Denmark and Iceland) own some companies. Sweden has 48 state-owned enterprises, Finland has 67, and Norway has 74. Norway owns 35% of the stocks on the Norwegian Stock Exchange. The Norwegian state owns a large part of the country's largest oil company Equinor (previously called Statoil), the country's largest telecommunications company Telenor, and the country's largest financial services group DNB. This would be like if the U.S. government owned ExxonMobil, Verizon, and JP Morgan Chase.

Finland's state ownership portfolio is less impressive but includes: the airline Finnair, the infrastructure engineering company VR, and the energy company Gasum. Finland's state also owns a few oddball enterprises like the public relations company Nordic Morning and, until earlier this year, the wine and spirits company Altia.

In the Nordic countries two-thirds of the wealth is in private hands—and they have more billionaires per million people than the U.S. does. Their economies are often called "state capitalism" rather than socialism—but the term commonly used for indicating some state ownership of the means of production is "socialism." This is not to be confused with the term "welfare state," although the two are often found together, especially in states with more welfare perks. But the capitalist U.S. also has some welfare programs (ie. public schools, Medicaid, Medicare, food stamps, and Social

Security). But while the U.S. pays for it by deferred taxation, such as borrowing, the Nordic countries pay for more of it by state ownership.

State ownership, like private ownership, can be highly effective--or a disaster. South Africa's major power company, Escom, is inefficient, mismanaged and corrupt. Norway's oil company, Equinor, is highly efficient and very profitable. On the private enterprise side, Enron and Lehman Brothers were large capitalist companies that "hit the fan." Private is not always better.

Why doesn't the U.S. pay for what it wants by increasing taxation or more state ownership? It is because of decades of capitalist propaganda which has permeated the American value system. It is so deeply ingrained that we don't even think about it. Take the idea of socialized medicine. Americans say, "I want to choose my own doctor." Propaganda!! I have never lived in a country with socialized medicine where I could not choose my own doctor. America's healthcare system is rated the 37th best in the world by the World Health Organization. It is also at least 40% more expensive than any other country's. Why is this? American doctors are the best paid. When everyone is covered, you don't need profit making insurance companies, answering to the stockholders with CEOs making ten figure incomes and vice presidents making over a million a year. And it wouldn't happen without multi-million dollar lobbying budgets—and intensive propaganda.

A GLANCE AT OTHER PRIORITIES

Is it good for the American people to spend more money on private prisons than on public university education? Why do we charge the best students for an education and make them borrow to pay for it? Maybe we should make prisoners borrow if they want to eat.

A U.S. Department of Education report showed that between 1979 and 2012, state and local government expenditures grew by 107% to $534 billion from $258 billion for elementary and secondary education, while corrections spending rose by 324% to $71 billion from $17 billion, the U.S. Department of Education report found. During that same period, the population of state and local corrections facilities surged more than four-fold to nearly 2.1 million from around 467,000, more than seven times the growth rate of the U.S. population overall. This was due in large part because of the widespread adoption of mandatory minimum sentence laws in the 1990s. Such laws were lobbied for by seven states - Idaho, Michigan, Montana, North Dakota, South Carolina, South Dakota and West Virginia - each exceeded the average rate, increasing their corrections spending five times as fast as they did their pre-kindergarten to grade 12 education spending.

In just two states, New Hampshire and Massachusetts, growth in corrections expenditures did not surpass elementary and secondary expenditures, even after accounting for changes in population.

State and local spending on postsecondary education has remained mostly flat since 1990, the report said. Average state and local per-capita spending on corrections increased by 44 percent while higher education funding per full-time equivalent student decreased by 28 percent, it said.

The United States spends about $80 billion a year on incarceration. 10 states spend more on prisons than on education. California is seen as the worst offender when it comes to spending more on corrections than education, and it's no wonder why: the state spent $9.6 billion on prisons in 2011, but just $5.7 billion on higher education. Overall, the state spends $8,667 for each student, but about $50,000 per inmate, per year. Vermont spent $111 million for prisons and $92 million on education. Pennsylvania spent $2.1 billion on prisons and $2 billion on education.

ALEC (the American Legislative Exchange Council) is an organization that develops model legislation that advances "free-market" principles such as privatization. Under their Criminal Justice Task Force, it has developed model bills that state legislators often consult when proposing "tough on crime" initiatives. These ideas are sponsored by private prison owners, who spend about $1.5 million a year on lobbying for longer and tougher sentencing—to keep their prisons packed and profitable. About forty states have passed laws based on ALEC's proposals.

Perhaps we are spending money unwisely, two-thirds of state prison inmates did not complete high school. A 10 percent increase in high school graduation rates would result in a 9 percent decline in criminal arrest rates. And education is cheaper! But privatization is the American way! Thank God we didn't have this problem in the 50s. My seven year education at UCLA was free! But, then, we didn't have privately operated prisons.

OUR EDUCATION RESULTS ARE POOR--WHY DON'T WE SEE THE TRUTH?

Is it really for "our good" that we have such a low level of educational achievement?
And, that we have the lowest rated, but most expensive, healthcare system of any developed country? Is it for the good of the American people to keep borrowing to fund our budgets, when we have put the country in a state of near bankruptcy. We have borrowed in good times and bad times—even though economists tell us to pay back during the good times.

Any informed person understands that one major problem is that so many Americans are not informed. The PISA scores comparing international education achievement in reading, mathematics and science, places Americans about 30 places away from the top countries-- China, Singapore, Estonia, Finland and many more. Why?

Could it be that our colonial based education network is so far behind the national systems of other countries that teaching up-to-date information with high-level educators is relatively rare? The average American teacher comes from the bottom 20% of college students. And, many of those colleges are very definitely sub-par. We have some truly outstanding schools in parts of California, Massachusetts, Connecticut and New York but they are too few in number. But educating young people to think for themselves would be a great danger to the capitalists and their legislative lackeys, who keep telling us, like Mitch McConnell that they are "for the good of the American people."

I don't know about you, but I am appalled by the number of people I see interviewed on television who say that they will make up their mind on who to vote for after they enter the voting booth. But their vote counts just as much as that of a person who has watched all the debates and read the platforms. It counts just as much as the vote of a Nobel Prize winner in economics. Are we voting for a party because our parents did--or our neighbors do? Is our vote dependent on the last political ad we saw or a fake news tidbit on Facebook or Twitter? Are we voting as if our lives depend on it? They often do!

WHAT ABOUT HAPPINESS?

Is it good for the American people to be far less happy than the Scandinavians? The USA is rated the 19th happiest country, in the current United Nations Annual

Happiness Survey. The Nordic countries are always in the top six. And the U.S. has been losing ground.

Is it good for the American people to continue to subsidize religions to the tune of hundreds of billions of dollars of lost tax money? Is it good for the American people to have a majority of the Supreme Court of one religion-- today it is Catholic.

Is it good for the American people to have elections financed by the capitalists rather than by the government? Is it good for the American people to be pitied and laughed at by the citizens of most of the other advanced countries? Is it good for the American people to have a government that denies the facts of global-warming. And there are so many other questions that we will look at in this book.

We need to have enough knowledge to be able to discern whether what we are hearing is real news and true, or fake news. We are continually bombarded with advertising and propaganda-- will we believe everything we see and hear? Do we? Our videogames and televisions will keep us entertained while the national powers ignore our best interests.

DO WE CARE?

If we care, we need to spend some time determining whether we want facts or fiction as the basis for our government. Are we going to put more stock in facts or faith? How are we going to look at how we fund our government? Are we going to look at whether the government makes laws in our interests or in the interests of the power elites—

> The selfish capitalists
> The government—executives, legislators and judges
> The military

Listing these three categories, following sociologist C. Wright Mills ideas, we must emphasize that the three categories are not all filled with bad guys. For example, Larry Page and Sergey Brin, the Google boys, have given us so much. I rather doubt that their original motivation was to become multi-billionaires. It just happened. I would guess that Bill Gates was also motivated by what he saw as a problem to be solved. His billions are now being used to fund many worthwhile projects. Warren Buffett, on the other hand, wanted to make millions. He exceeded his expectations. These are only three of the "good" capitalists. In the government and in the military we have many thousands of good people. The problem is that in each of these elite groups we have power-hungry people who are pursuing their basic psychological drive for power. The huge majority of us have this same drive, but we have often tempered it with love—as the welfare state countries have.

There is no simple sugar-coated way to understand the problems we face. We must be clear in our definitions or we will not be talking about the same thing. When we say "God is good" or "democracy is good" what do we mean by "God," " democracy," or "good?" Very simple questions but the answers to each of them are multifaceted and extensive.

PROPAGANDA

We often believe what see, hear, and read. Our positive or negative evaluation of that sensory input will depend on the quality and extensiveness of our formal education and our other experiences in traveling, business, reading, and keeping up to date with truthful news reports and well thought out editorial pieces. A well-traveled Yale graduate should have different criteria for judging a piece of information than a high school drop-out in Alabama whose travel experience is limited to his occasional trips to the mailbox!

We should know where and why we stand along the political spectrum, the religious belief continuum, and in our own life priorities.

Part of this book is devoted to finding where we stand, part on how to spot errors in the propaganda that inundates us, and part in attempting to understand more deeply the political and economic issues we face—and where we want to go.

So, for those of you who want to look a little deeper into our present and our future, bear with me as we start at the beginning-- which I find is a good place to start.

We will start with looking at ourselves and getting us on the same page in terms of definitions, understanding the different values that people live by, and how these factors place us on different parts of the political spectrum, from the violent reactionary right, through the right-leaning conservative, through the left-leaning liberal, to the violent left side of the spectrum. As part of this section, we will look at the techniques that propagandists or uninformed people use to convince us to believe what they want us to.

Then we will look at some of the possibilities open to us in the political and economic spheres to improve our governments and our lives.

From there on—it's up to you. Will you vote differently? Will you become politically active? How active? **It's your life, your country, your world!**

# PART I

## UNDERSTANDING HOW WE THINK

Our minds are the filters of what we learn and what we know. They are our engines of energy that thrust our beings into our adult lives. They accept values to guide them—values sometimes absorbed, sometimes deliberated.

But how true is what we "know?" Opinions are worthless unless they correspond with reality. The messages we hear that are designed to influence us are propaganda. But is that propaganda true, partially true, or totally false? The strength of our belief does not make it more true! "I believe in God." "Abortion is murder." "Democracy is the only intelligent system of government." "Capital punishment is immoral." All of these ideas are held strongly by some, and opposed just as strongly by others.

A belief in God or in democracy really is a factual question. But before investigating their truth or falsity, we must define **exactly** what we mean by "God" or "democracy."

The other two beliefs, concerning abortion or capital punishment, are values. Whether or not they are values to be followed, depends on the assumptions we use to form our values, then on the evidence that backs up our position. How have we learned or established our values—have we learned them at mother's knee, from the preacher's pulpit, or from our teacher's mouth? Sometimes we change our values because of new friends, other times by thinking our way into new values.

As an example of the combination of values and lies, Donald Trump's self-centered value of being reelected in 2020 prompted his re-election committee to paint Joe Biden as 'the opposition' in the coronavirus war. While Trump's preparation for and handling of the COVID-19 pandemic was one of the worst in the world, rivalling Sweden's inept response, the majority of the American public was not aware of the superior preparation and response of most of the developed countries. They listened to his press conferences and seemed to forget his "rosey" predictions on the outcome--as thousands of Americans died, including health-care workers—who did not have enough masks or protective equipment. And for those infected, not enough ventilators. Few knew that he had eliminated the White House office that was charged with preparing for pandemics--because it saved money. In spite of his ineptness, his popularity ratings hit all-time highs, near 50%.

But never let a major world crisis be wasted! How can it be turned against a political rival? Effective propaganda, that's how! So, his election committee recommended painting the Democrats, and Biden in particular, as being responsible for the problem—saying that the impeachment proceedings delayed preparing for the pandemic, and that Biden was doing nothing to help.

In this section we will attempt to explore the ways to challenge our minds to sort out the truth from the falsity of the ideas that the capitalist and political propagandists would have us believe.

# CHAPTER 2

## WHAT DO WE MEAN BY WHAT WE SAY?

We can't understand each other unless we are talking about the exact same thing. In political thinking, philosophy, and religions, as well as many other areas, we need to define our major ideas. In philosophy, this is called the study of semantics. We will touch on this later in the book.

Four hundred years ago the philosopher Thomas Hobbes observed that everyone is content with his own amount of common sense. Today we might paraphrase that and say that everyone is content with his or her amount of knowledge. It doesn't matter the source of that knowledge—The Times of London, Wall Street Journal, Fox News, one's friends, or CNN.

Our current American thinking is not new. It seems to go back at least 200 years. In 1835, the English translation of Alexis de Tocqueville's "Democracy in America" was printed. He had visited America on behalf of the French government on another task, but he did his own sociological and political studies while he was there. One of his observations was that,
"I know of no country in which there is so little independence of mind and real freedom of discussion as in America." (Democracy in America) We shall revisit de Tocqueville periodically through the text. It seems that we are more geared by tradition, and less by logic, than we might believe.

### WHAT DO WE MEAN?

When we say "democracy" do we mean one person one vote? Do we mean a republican form of government like most advanced countries have today—with democratically elected representatives making the laws? Do we mean a country that allows a great many human rights—or human desires? Do we mean a country that is guided by equality primarily or by liberty primarily? So, let's look at a few definitions that will be used and how we will use them.

Economic systems are the systems of government that produce the wealth. They can be any combination of: a feudal economy with part of the production going to the king or noble. It may be a slave economy, where unpaid people produce a good part of the wealth. It can be capitalism, where much of the profit goes to the people who built the factories. It should not be confused with political systems which involve the choice of the leaders and the workings of the government.

### THE PRODUCERS OF WEALTH

LABORERS—work for wages, or other rewards, with their bodies or brains, following traditional knowledge or instructions to obtain a desired result.

CAPITALISTS—earn money on their money. They may, or may not be involved in managing the business. Stockholders and bankers are examples.

ENTREPRENUERS—create wealth with novel ideas, sometimes with novel business ideas, sometimes undertaking a traditional business in a new way. The entrepreneur is self-motivated, but may take money from capitalists to fund the early years of the business.

Bill Gates, Thomas Edison and the 'Google boys" were entrepreneurs, who eventually became capitalists. To the degree that they remained creative in the business they could be considered entrepreneurial-capitalists. Warren Buffet, on the other hand, seems to have been a capitalist all his business life, since he was dealing primarily in stocks and companies.

GOVERNMENTS—can act as capitalists or entrepreneurs. The NASA space program is a prime example of entreprenuering, and the Norwegian or Saudi oil exploration and extraction are examples of the state being the capitalist.

## ECONOMIC SYSTEMS

A few are:

Hunting and gathering-- where the family or society is in a pre-agricultural economic system.

Agricultural-- where the society can remain in one place because they have to learn to till the soil.

Feudal-- where the owner of the property allows people to work and takes part of their produce as rent.

Simple manufacturing and trade-- where crafts, like baskets or pottery, are traded.

Capitalism-- where the manufacturing is financed and controlled by the people with money (capital).

Socialism-- a system in which the government owns part of the industry, with the profits that the capitalist had previously pocketed going to the government. This is used in welfare states to help pay the government's bills, but government ownership is also used by some monarchies, such as the UAE and Saudi Arabia, with the profits going to the emirs or the king,

Communism-- a system where the government owns all of the means of production. In Marx's development of communist theory, the people would own all the means of production.

Modern advanced economic systems are generally a combination of socialism and capitalism.

## POLITICAL TERMS

If we are to intelligently discuss how we want to be governed, we must use the same meanings as the people with whom we are discussing. We also must be able to decipher what capitalists and politicians are telling us—is it true or is it false propaganda.

Populism—has traditionally meant anti-establishment or anti-intellectual political movements or philosophies that offer unorthodox solutions or policies and appeal to the common person rather than according with traditional party or partisan ideologies. It often advocates more egalitarianism for the working class or the common person. It thus would be on the left side of the political spectrum. So when Bernie Sanders is referred to as a populist, it follows the traditional definition. But Donald Trump, a reactionary, has also been called a populist. This is probably because he has appealed to lower social class people in his anti-immigration and anti-abortion stances. So, a word which once meant anti-establishment, now seems to mean only "popular with some lower social class people."

Other terms, such as liberal, conservative, fascism, socialism and communism will be dealt with in great detail in the next several pages.


## POLITICAL VALUES

Major political values deal with who will have the power, the source of the power, and how it will be used. The major political values are'

EQUALITY

Equality means exactly the same. So two equals two, it doesn't equal 2.001. By this definition, no two people who ever lived are equal physically and mentally. The only way that we can find that people are actually equal is if they have souls that are actually equal. If the soul is in the image of God and God is infinite, people could be equal. But this idea rests on the realities of a concept which is relatively new.

The traditional Christian idea stems from Thomas Aquinas's interpretation of Aristotle who believed that we had an animal soul which was originally equal but it became unequal as the person lived. For those who believe in equality based on an equal soul, they have to base it on unverifiable theological grounds—such as: there is a creating Supernatural and that Creator put equal spiritual souls in each of us-- from a saint to a serial killer.

You may look at the Declaration of Independence and see that Thomas Jefferson wrote that "all men are created equal." It is highly doubtful that Jefferson believed this, and if so, it would be based on John Locke's idea that we are born with a mind with nothing on it-- a blank slate, a tabula rasa. There would be no genetic potentials and no epigenetic influences. This, then, would be counter to what science has discovered about the brain and the mind.

If we can believe Jefferson's own writings, he did not believe in a theistic God who judged people and sent them to heaven or hell. He said that he believed in a deistic god who created the world but is not involved in the operation of the world. In actuality, Jefferson was trying to get the Americans to revolt against the King of England. Whenever people want to revolt against the ruling powers, they say that they are equal to the ruling powers. So the Declaration of Independence is neither a law nor a statement of fact. It is a call to rebellion.

Even if we are not equal in fact, we may be better served in a society in which we act somewhat equally. In the ancient Athens, when they developed the idea of a democracy, it was only the free men who were allowed to be equal in a vote. Neither women, children nor slaves were permitted the vote so it was actually a minority of the population that were considered equal enough to vote.

The idea of democracy, as it has developed from the revolutions in America and France, has given rise to offering more equality in a society than simply the right to an equal vote. In the 19th century, Karl Marx took the idea to a very high level, counting everyone's needs as equal being essential for the society. In the 20th century, the American philosopher John Dewey, said that while we are not actually equal, society works better if we are treated somewhat equally. When there is too much difference between the top and the bottom, revolution may be considered as it was in the 18th century by America and France.

More recently, equality has become a standard of justice. The justice theory of John Rawls and the economic theory of Thomas Piketty are based on a strong belief in the reality of equality as a basis for society. Piketty recommends a series of reforms. They include:

> a schedule of taxation on income and wealth as high as 90%,
> the elimination of nation-states and national borders, with free movement of people,
> a trans-national democracy,
> a universal right to education.

The European Union has developed its Convention on Human Rights with a major emphasis on equality and equal rights. The European Union's Court of Equal Justice goes even farther in its interpretation of equality and equal rights. In one case, the court overruled the British courts in allowing a convicted murderer, serving a life sentence, to have a child with his wife whom he met when she was also a prisoner. In another case, it overruled the British courts in allowing a terrorist to return to England and take up residence there.

An example of people being treated equally comes from Norway. In 1991 a Kurd known as Mullah Krekar was given asylum in the country. He served a number of prison terms, for such things as threatening the Prime Minister. Norway was paying all his legal expenses. In 2007 he was listed as a terrorist by the United Nations. A few years later he was sentenced to death, in absentia, by an Iraqi court. Norway refused to extradite him because of their opposition to the death penalty. With the EU, Norway sees everyone as equally deserving to live. In 2020 they did deport him to Italy which had found him guilty of another terrorist related crime.

Running a truly equalitarian society may cost the society a great deal of money to deal with anti-social individuals. Critics have said that the money could be better spent helping law-abiding needy citizens in their country—or in other countries. The economic burden of enforcing equalitarian treatment may be a consideration for the future.

It should be noted that equal rights are not necessarily related to the equality of the individual people. They are actually primarily based on freedom-- on liberty and on equality of opportunity, which is primarily a basic requirement-- if diversity is to be achieved.

LIBERTY

Liberty means having freedom. But how much freedom? The philosopher Immanuel Kant said that the basis for ethics was that we should never use another person as a means to our own ends. Sometimes we hear it said that "your freedom stops and my nose."

The American Constitution gives us freedom of speech. What the Founding Fathers meant was the freedom to speak political ideas. But, just as in gun rights, where the Supreme Court has changed the meaning of the original Constitution, freedom of speech is now allowed in nearly every area. In Europe, by contrast, hate speech is not allowed.

Freedom is often amplified to include "license"-- by that I mean, the freedom to do what one will in spite of negative social consequences. The Supreme Court, in Brandenburg v. Ohio, 395 U.S. 444 (1969), allowed the Ku Klux Klan in Ohio to speak at a rally, in which in one speech it was suggested to have, "revengeance" against "Niggers," "Jews," and those who supported them. (If you haven't heard the word "revengeance," it is because there is no such word—but it sure sounds nasty, coming from an illiterate klansman!)

One of the speeches also claimed that "our President, our Congress, our Supreme Court, continue to suppress the white, Caucasian race," and announced plans for a march on Washington to take place on the Fourth of July. Brandenburg was charged with advocating violence under Ohio's criminal syndicalism statute for his participation in the rally and for the speech he made.

The Court held that the government cannot punish inflammatory speech unless that speech is "directed to inciting or producing imminent lawless action and is likely to incite or produce such action." The decision struck down several previous court decisions. Analysts now assume that if you don't want to hurt or kill a person in the next few minutes, it seems to be acceptable.

One might think that the Court would consider the "legislative intent" of the law, the Constitution, in considering its ruling. Courts do consider legislative intent when it backs up the decision they want to make. If they want to make a new law, they can't be bothered! No law in America has its legislative intent more clearly stated than does the Constitution in its Preamble:

***We the People*** of the United States, in Order to form a more perfect Union, establish Justice, insure domestic Tranquility, provide for the common defence, promote the general Welfare, and secure the Blessings of Liberty to ourselves and our Posterity, do ordain and establish this Constitution for the United States of America.

Some may wonder how hate speech "insures domestic tranquility" or "promotes the general welfare." I am one of them!

But the Supreme Court, in Jacobson v. Massachusetts, 197 U.S. 11 (1905), ruled that: "The United States does not derive any of its substantive powers from the Preamble of the Constitution. It cannot exert any power to secure the declared objects of the Constitution unless, apart from the Preamble, such power be found in, or can properly be implied from, some express delegation in the instrument."

While courts are supposed to look at the letter of the law and the intent of the legislature in developing that law, the English and American concept of "common law" allows the judges to become legislators. This does not happen under the Napoleonic law that is used in most countries, where the letter of the law, and its legislative intent, are primary. If this were true in United States, the Preamble to the Constitution would be considered to be fundamental to the interpretation of the various elements of the Constitution. But the courts have consistently held that the Preamble has no effect of law. So, the phrase "to promote the general welfare" does not affect the interpretation of a law, and it seems also to not have any effect in regard to the legislative intent of the Founding Fathers.

In America, some legislatures and some courts have allowed their religious beliefs to influence American law and to reduce the freedom of the people even when that freedom is both good for the society and individual. As an example, the freedom of choice to have an abortion is eliminated in some jurisdictions even though the world is overpopulated and every new human body increases the carbon dioxide output to continue the global warming. The average carbon footprint of a person is 20 metric tons (44,000 pounds) of carbon dioxide per year. Then their children would also increase the impact on climate change. Also, children born who are not wanted, are susceptible to criminality and mental illness. This is clearly shown in numerous scientific studies.

## EQUALITY OF OPPORTUNITY

Here we have a meeting of the ideals of equality and liberty. The concept is that people may start with equal opportunities but then their intelligence, work ethic and education will determine their level of achievement. The Universal Declaration of Human Rights of the United Nations and the European Union's Convention on Human Rights both emphasize equality of opportunity and the liberty to follow one's chosen path. The Universal Declaration of Human Rights ends with some duties to the society for the citizens as required to have a functioning society. The European Union's Convention on Human Rights does not require any duties of the individual to the society.

Therefore, if we are to have true equality of opportunity for the citizens, which should also advance the society, a rethinking of the selfishness that permeates all societies, particularly the capitalist societies, is necessary. If the individual is to be given the liberty to achieve and, possibly, to financially profit from his or her industry. True equality of opportunity cannot be achieved unless every individual starts equally and with equal opportunities. Since people in power—financial, legislative, judicial, military and business—control societies, and most hold their selfish motivations paramount, major obstacles to the equality of opportunity exist. Necessary requirements for true equality of opportunity will be opposed by those power elites. Among the requirements are: a 100% tax on inheritance and equal opportunities for high level education being available to all throughout their lives. The strong probability is that the self-centeredness of the elites will never be extinguished in a democratic republic. The possibility that true equality of opportunity, as posited by Plato, can ever be realized as long as the elites control the minds of the voters, and the level of education in the country is mediocre.

Control by the legislatures and the courts is unlikely to change the existing systems to emulate the ideas of Plato which would result in a more just and functioning society. Our psychological natures, geared to our power drives and our parochial selfishness continue to overpower a logical approach to individual and societal accomplishment.

## FUNCTIONS OF GOVERNMENT

With the great 18$^{th}$ century revolutions, we found that both prince and pontiff weighed too heavily on our potentials, so a government should allow for liberty.

To allow liberty—because people are physically and mentally unequal, and they are unequal in their willingness to work, liberty has been an essential element in constitutional democracies the last few hundred years. The American Constitution guarantees only certain rights of liberty. The Declaration of Independence, which some mistake for an American guarantee of equality, was a call to revolution. In calling for revolution, the revolutionaries emphasize that they want equality with the controlling governmental powers. The American Constitution, which is the country's fundamental law, never mentions equality. On the other hand, the French Declaration of the Rights of Man mentions equality three times.

Modern democracies and democratic ethical systems have, however, emphasized equality, at the expense of liberty. Welfare state benefits provide for equality in their socialized health care, democratic voting, and unemployment benefits, and often in their opposition to the death penalty. They provide for liberty, primarily through equality of opportunities, in free education through the doctorate, more paid vacation time, parental care leave, early childhood education, and often euthanasia.

## FINANCIAL REALITIES TO PAY FOR OUR GOVERNMENT

**Governments may support themselves these three ways:**

- **Immediate taxing--of their incomes, sales, property, etc.**
- **Delayed taxing--by borrowing or devaluing their currency**
- **Socialism--by partial government ownership of some industries**

In the U.S. we use the first two, because we are one of the most capitalistic countries in the world. Still, we are rated 19$^{th}$ in the United Nations' annual happiness ratings and 23$^{rd}$ in our perception of corruption in government. Might that be because capitalists spend millions of dollars annually to get legislators to enact into law what they want, like lower taxes and fewer regulations designed to allow them to ignore the well-being of the citizens?

Nearly 200 years ago Alexis de Tocqueville observed that, "A democratic government is the only one in which those who vote for a tax can escape the obligation to pay it. (Democracy in America, Chapter 13)

And regarding government ownership, the happiest countries borrow less, but use some degree of socialism—allowing earnings, that would go to individuals in the U.S., to be used for the general good—a welfare state. For example, during the corona virus scare, Norway was loaning companies money at very low rates, or taking stock in those companies. The money came from its trillion dollar savings account earned from the government owned oil company. The account was to be used to guarantee pensions and when needed by the state—such as the economic crisis that grew out of the COVID-19 pandemic. On the other side of the Atlantic, the U.S. had to borrow the funds it needed, indebting every American another $6060. So much for state ownership!

CHAPTER 3
## IS WHAT IS BEING SAID TRUE?
## CAN WE SEPARATE FACT FROM FAITH AND FAKE?

We are continually being bombarded by information—some true, some partially true, and some blatantly false. Advertisers, politicians, friends, people with varying motives—sometimes sinister, and foreign governments have the abilities and the means of delivery to make their messages heard. It is more important than ever to be able to sort out the truths from the lies and rationalizations we continually hear.

> ➢ Is the Tesla really the best car for the future?
> ➢ Is the cause of your friend's divorce really what your divorcing friend says it was, or is there more to the story?
> ➢ Can deep breathing really prevent you from catching a corona virus?

When people have a psychological problem, like narcissism, and they have been found to have made a mistake, they rationalize or lie. In rationalizing, they think it is the truth, but it is not. In lying, the person knows it is not the truth—but they want you to think it is.

So we are continually being bombarded with messages. How do we discern what is true and what is false? The discipline of philosophy, in its area of "logic" it has given us rules to understand what is meant in a word, phrase, or argument. (This is "semantics.") It has given us the tools to determine the truth or falsity of a statement. (This is "inductive logic" and the obstacles to analyzing the truth, "inductive fallacies.") Then when you know what is meant, and whether or not it is true, there are rules for making an argument valid, whether the conclusion follows from the premises. (This is "deductive logic.")

## SEMANTICS

We must know what we mean by what we say. We must understand what the speaker means when we hear a statement. Finding the exact meaning of words and phrases is the area of philosophy called semantics. When we say, "there is a God," exactly what do we mean by "God?" Is it the sun, as the ancient Egyptians believed? Is it the vengeful God of the pre-Christian era? Is it a merciful God? Is it a being that this concerned with how we act? Thomas Jefferson, and other founding fathers, believed in a "deistic" creating God that was not concerned with those of us in the world. The Christians, Jews, and Muslims believe in a God that judges and rewards or punishes. The ancient Greeks and Romans believed in a number of supernatural beings. Exactly what do you mean by "God" and what does your minister, neighbor, or president mean? When pushed to explain thoroughly the concept of God, we will have innumerable definitions.

The same is true of the concept of democracy. Some will emphasize the ideal of equality, others of liberty, for others it will be the economic system of capitalism. In Scandinavia they will define it as a combination of socialism and capitalism with an emphasis on the welfare state. So, what we mean by a term must be understood by the people or person with whom I am discussing. If we do not agree to what we are talking about, there is no real discussion, so we are wasting our time.

It seems that many are not interested in being precise in the words they choose:

- ➤ "It's cold as hell." From what I have read in Paradise Lost and the Qur'an, Hell is a very hot place!
- ➤ My fuk'n car won't start. Could it be tired from its all night auto-orgy? Or. Are you certain that it was fuk'n. or are you lying?
- ➤ "You mothafuker." Are you certain of the incestual proclivities of your adversary?
- ➤ "God damn you, you stupid dog." Do you really want your dog to go to Hell forever? And how do you know that he has an immortal soul?

Some use a word like "fuck" as a noun, verb, adjective, adverb or interjection. It saves them from thinking and being precise with their meaning. Of course, having a coarse connotation, makes us appear tougher—so it helps to soothe our inferiority feelings and gives us a boost in our need for psychological power. Who would have guessed that such an old Germanic-English word would serve us so well in today's world—and that it could be such a stumbling block to intelligent thinking!

**IS IT TRUE?**

A second area of logic is called inductive logic. Here we look at how probable is the truth of your statement. Having an opinion does not make it true, but of course your opinion may be true. If you say "all Mexicans are illegal immigrants." This is of course false because there are millions of people from Mexico who are American citizens. Some may be only American citizens, others may hold dual citizenship. Remember that the southwestern states of the USA, from Texas to California, were owned by Mexico prior to the 1840s. So the ancestors of many Hispanics were in the southwestern part of the U.S. long before the Anglos arrived.

The US went to war to aggressively gain a great deal of Mexican territory. I'll bet the Mexicans wish they had built a wall from northern California across to Colorado and down to Texas before the war. Even if they had paid for it themselves, they would be way ahead financially!

So, we are looking at the argument, and not who said it. Very often we assume something is true because of who said it: the Pope, the President. the king, the candidate. What is the probability that United Kingdom will be better off since it has left the EU? What was the probability that invading Iraq and getting rid of Saddam Hussein would give birth to ISIS? What is the probability that Donald Trump can make America safer?

There are always people who are not happy with all that the government is doing. They may want: better primary education, better roads, free college tuition, a war with Iran, higher taxes on the rich, lower taxes, higher wages, better and cheaper healthcare, and a number of other wishes. No government can make everyone happy, so in every election cycle there is the opportunity for the "out" politicians to promise the moon. When the "ins" haven't delivered it, we vote back in the rascals we voted out in the last election.

It is standard political procedure to play on the anger and disappointment of the population and promise them hope, if they will vote for you. In the West, in recent times, we have had some semblance of rationality in the political discourse. In the last several years we have had George W. Bush, Brexit, and Donald J. Trump strike down rational thinking and promise us things that sound good but are highly detrimental to our nations.

**TALK ABOUT UNINFORMED VOTERS**

- ➤40 percent of Trump voters insist that he won the national popular vote.

➢60 percent of Trump voters think that Hillary Clinton received millions of illegal votes.

➢ 73 percent of Trump voters believe that George Soros is paying anti-Trump protesters.

➢29 percent of Trump voters don't think California votes should be allowed to count in the national popular vote.

➢67 percent of Trump voters think the unemployment rate went up under President Barack Obama. Only 20 percent accurately believe it went down. (9.4% to 4.7%)

➢39 percent of Trump voters think the stock market went down under Obama. And 19 percent are unsure. (Under Obama the Dow went up from 7949 to 19827, it rose 150%, to match Obama's gain the DOJ average would have to end at 49369 under Trump. Today it is at 22,600.)

➢14 percent of Trump voters think Hillary Clinton was connected to a child sex ring run out of a Washington pizzeria. Another 32 percent aren't sure one way or another. Only 54 percent are certain that Pizzagate was a myth.

Millions of people vote straight party lines or they vote on information that is not correct. Those who believed Trump, were believing statements that were found to be 50% totally false, 20% mostly false, and less than 20% of what he said was true or partially true. There was plenty of publicity on the truth and falsity of the statements by both presidential candidates, but the Rust Belt voters either didn't know or didn't care. What does this say about intelligent voting in our democracy?

People who want to lead a nation or to vote intelligently for representatives need much more information today than ever before. We need an extensive knowledge of world history, macroeconomics, natural science, biological science, the theory of science, philosophy of religion, comparative religions, political science along with some knowledge of psychology and sociology and an understanding of ethics. Armed with a strong background in basic knowledge we can then effectively criticize or agree with propositions that are held by candidates who want to run our governments.

Donald Trump is an anti-intellectual politician. He has little knowledge or regard for science. He changes his position on major issues from week to week, possibly depending on the audience he is addressing. Changing a position is not wrong if you have additional evidence to make you change your mind. Ethically it is wrong if you're only changing it for political motives and do not plan to follow through with policies that implement your position.

About a month after taking office Trump cited a Muslim terror incident in Sweden two days prior. The fact is that there never was such an incident, it was a fabrication. When asked about it he said that someone had told him. He did not name the someone. Conversely, less than a week later an article appeared in the New York Times from an unknown source that criticized him. He insisted on the source being named. This waffling back and forth based on his actions and words and how they are reported and negatively impact on him has created not only concerns but also a number of questions about his psychological health.

There are a large number of fallacies that relate to inductive logic. Often, they are not used to deceive, but the arguer has opinions that do not stand up to scrutiny. When Tea Party advocates were "definitely" against socialism, but could not define what it was that they were against, it was just ignorance-- not malice.

Other vacations from truth include: lies, since they are known to be false by the liar; and rationalizations (reasons given for behavior that are not true but are believed to be true by the person giving the excuse). They are merely psychological blinders that hide an uncomfortable truth.

HOW DO THEY TRY TO FOOL US?

The study of logic has categorized a number ways that people may try to fool us. These are called inductive fallacies and they have been used extensively lately. We will give you an abbreviated list to give you an idea of how so many magicians of the mouth have attempted to pull the wool over our brains in their quests for political power.

When listening to candidates who are attempting to become elected today, we often hear statements that are not true, fake news, and promises that are impossible to fulfill. Many of these can be analyzed in terms of their truth or falsity. Many of these are what we call "logical fallacies." Here are just a few illustrations.

One common type of fallacy is called an **argumentum ad hominem**. (The argument is false because of the person who said it.)

Donald Trump criticized former Florida governor Jeb Bush in this way several times. He said that Bush: "had no honor," "was a hypocrite," "has no clue," and a number of other epithets that had nothing to do with the arguments that Bush was making. At various times, he called him: sad, desperate, a total disaster, a low energy guy, a sad sack, a low energy stiff and in many other negatives without criticizing his arguments. Bush was a major candidate with good credentials but was embarrassed out of the primary race.

Among the positions that Jeb Bush had taken were:
➢No litmus test for judicial appointees,
➢Abortion OK if the life of the mother was at risk,
➢Defund Planned Parenthood,
➢Aim for 4% national economic growth,
➢Bank bailouts were necessary,
➢For a balanced-budget,
➢Let businesses express religious freedom against homosexuals,
➢Lower tax rates on businesses,
➢For school vouchers,
➢A skeptic on global warming.

These conservative or reactionary positions actually agreed with Trump on many of the conservative-reactionary Republican positions. If an intelligent debate were going to be accomplished they needed to argue about those areas in which they disagreed. Instead Bush was personally attacked, but his issues were not discussed.

Trump called US Senator Marco Rubio "a lightweight" 19 times that I counted.

On John Kasich, the Governor of Ohio Trump called him: a typical politician, poor, doesn't have what it takes, can't debate, dummy, one of the worst presidential candidates in history, a total failure, so easy to beat, total dud, pathetic.

Trump's major approach to winning the primaries and the general election was in criticizing his opponents, usually without any proof. While this is not sound, as an inductive argument, it works because so many people are primarily moved by their unconscious minds and their inferiority complexes. It makes us feel good when somebody else is put down. And research often shows that when you hear something about 20 times—you generally accept it as true.

Another type of logical fallacy is the **"argument from ignorance."** In this line of thinking the person claims that something is true because it cannot be disproven. This is an argument often used in religion to prove God. Trump said he could increase the Gross Domestic Product by 3% and maybe as high as 6%. The first quarter growth in 2017 was only 1.2%, the lowest in three years. For the year, it was 2.3%. Then in 2018 it topped 3% for a couple of quarters, ending at 1% for the last quarter, In 2019 it was pretty steady at 2.1%. Of course, in 2020 it tanked because of the corona virus.

In the UK, Brexit voters were told that their economy would improve. Their 2017 GDP rise was 1.5%, lowest of all EU countries—which averaged a 2.7% gain for the year. Oh well, ignorance!

Another type of fallacy is called **"the appeal to the stone."** Here, someone else's argument is dismissed because I say so, without any proof. I counted 27 times that Trump called Ted Cruz a liar. He also called him a number of other negatives like: hypocrite, not nice, cheater, nasty, desperate, and a big problem.

Ted Cruz had many of the same views as Trump. He was a free-trade advocate, against abortion, for gun rights, against the Affordable Care Act, hard line on immigration, denied climate change, and saw Iran as an enemy.

He did vary from Trump in advocating a flat income tax and abolishing the IRS, and being against a higher minimum wage, Cruz also proposed eliminating the departments of: Energy, Education, Commerce, Housing and Urban Development. Should these issues have been discussed, or was it enough to forget them? Here we have a combination of dismissing the arguments because of who said them (ad hominem fallacy) and because Trump said so.

On the corona virus pandemic, throughout late February, Trump continued to claim that the situation was improving. On February 26, he said: "We're going down, not up. We're going very substantially down, not up." On February 27, he predicted: "It's going to disappear. One day — it's like a miracle — it will disappear." On February 29th, he said a vaccine would be available "very quickly" and "very rapidly" and praised his administration's actions as "the most aggressive taken by any country." None of these claims were true.

Instead, he suggested on multiple occasions that the virus was less serious than the flu. "We're talking about a much smaller range" of deaths than from the flu, he said on March 2. "It's very mild," he told Sean Hannity, of Fox News, on March 4. On March 7, he said, "I'm not concerned at all." On March 10, he promised: "It will go away. Just stay calm. It will go away."

Liberty University President Jerry Falwell Jr. showed up on *Fox & Friends* to explain that North Korean and Chinese scientists created the virus; a notion that none of the show's uninformed hosts felt compelled to challenge. Of course, it was a totally false statement from the reverend.

Sometimes fallacies are implied. For example, what is called the **anecdotal fallacy** deals with a personal experience that is supposed to counter the available evidence. Since Donald Trump was worth over $3 billion he must've been successful. That success in business would obviously carryover to success in government. Of course, there is no evidence of this would happen--only conjecture. (Actually, businessmen who have become presidents have been among our least effective presidents. We'll come to that in a few moments.)

In 2020 Trump brought up his uncle, John Trump, who taught at MIT. He then stated that because his uncle was so smart, so was he. As smart as Donald is, he should know that knowledge is not carried in the genes. It is in books and scientific articles that should have been read yesterday. Apparently, no president in history has disregarded provable facts anywhere near as much as Donald Trump, his statements will be used extensively to indicate some of the fallacies that run counter to verifiable scientific or historical facts.

There is also the "**appeal the probability**" fallacy. Here the arguer postulates that this would probably be the case. In the Brexit campaign, it was held that a return to sovereignty by leaving the EU would bring all sorts of positive effects. Trump's slogan "to make America great again," somehow assumed that the United States was not great even though it was the world's greatest economic power and it had the world's greatest military force. Trump gave no reasons why the country was not great, although we can assume that it meant that we needed more coal mining and steelmaking jobs.

In a tweet on February 24, 2020 Trump wrote, "The coronavirus is very much under control in the USA. We are in contact with everyone and all relevant countries. CDC & World Health have been working hard and very smart. Stock Market starting to look very good to me!" But the number of corona cases when he tweeted was 19 in the U.S., five weeks later it was 312,000 cases and 8,500 deaths. And the stock market Dow-Jones average dropped from about 29,000 on tweet-day to about 21,000 in the four-week period. Oops!

The" **conjunction fallacy**" assumes that if one outcome is probable, so are many others. Trump made his case for "making America great again," this one slogan was supposed to carry over into creating jobs for coal miners and steelworkers, cutting down the murder rates in Chicago, moving illegal immigrants back to their home countries, cutting taxes for the rich, and marginalizing Muslims.

Then there is the type of fallacy that tries to link a possible positive outcome to a previous but unrelated positive outcome. It can also be used to link a negative outcome to a possible negative outcome. For example, claiming that Hillary Clinton was responsible for the killing of an ambassador in Benghazi, which she was not, would therefore make her unreliable as a president. Clinton could have brought up the more than a thousand cases in which Trump was a defendant. Some of these were cases involving federal laws which he had violated. Some were cases in which he did not pay his contractors.

When Hillary was asked why she didn't attack him the way he attacked her she said that, Michelle Obama had told her that "when they go low, we go high." She assumed that a higher level of ethical behavior would win when contrasted with his baseless fallacies. She was wrong. Most people say they want ethics in government, but the truth is that for many, their most basic needs and their need to fulfill their power drives is primary when it comes to voting. In the future politicians should say, "when they go low, we will go lower."

There is another type of "ad hominem" argument which is called "**poisoning the well**." If Hillary had done anything wrong in the past, she would do everything wrong in the future. This is without proving that anything was wrong with her emails or the Benghazi situation. (She was cleared of wrongdoing in both cases.) Trump continued to bring these up as if they were major concerns for a future president. Another type of this argument is to abuse the arguer rather than answer the argument. This has been a major approach of Donald Trump.

One consequence seems to be emerging: "Almost everywhere, the populist right is trying to blame the contagion on open borders and migrants." Far-right politicians in Italy, France, Germany, and Spain have all jumped on the virus to call for tighter immigration policies. Some irrational thinking has accompanied that trend: A Fox News host, for example, "explained that the world was suffering from this epidemic because the Chinese Communist Party cannot feed its people, who have resorted, he claimed, to 'eating raw bats and snakes,'" This, of course, was also false!

After reading a headline from an outlet with a history of spreading false conspiracy theories, Trump said, "Johnson & Johnson to create coronavirus vaccine." It was totally false.

Another common fallacy is called **incredulity** that is a lack of belief. If I don't believe something, it can't be true.

Trump did not believe that the Obamacare health program was any good. Of course, he did not understand that what Obama wanted and what he got from Congress were two very different programs. When Trump worked to get a healthcare program through the House of Representatives, he said, "who knew that healthcare could be so complicated!"

Still another fallacy is called the **argument from silence**. Here my argument must be true because there is no evidence against it. I am a good businessman therefore I will be a good president. There is no evidence against this since I am not aware of any. Actually, the evidence is that in the US in the last hundred years, businessmen have been among our worst presidents.

Of the 44 presidents that preceded Donald Trump, the American Political Science Association rates only two businessmen in the top half of presidents. Harry Truman rates 6$^{th}$ and George H.W. Bush at 17$^{th}$. The others were: Warren Harding at 44, Herbert Hoover at 38, George W. Bush at 35, Calvin Coolidge at 27, and Jimmy Carter at 26. But all had had some experience in state or national governments. Truman had been a Senator and Vice President. Bush a Congressman, Vice President and Ambassador to the United Nations. Harding had also been a US Senator and was Lieutenant Governor of Ohio. Coolidge had been Vice President. Hoover had been Secretary of Commerce. Donald Trump is the only President who had only business experience.

Another fallacy is called **equivocation**. Here a word, with more than one meaning, is used to confuse the issue. For example, when creationists say that "evolution is only a theory" they are confusing a common use of the word with the scientific use of the word "theory"-- which means an established highly probable idea based on extensive research. Einstein's theories of relativity are examples. The creationists are using a different definition of theory which really means just guessing. "I have a theory that if I bet on black on the roulette wheel five times I will win at least twice."

"Let's make America great again." What does "great" actually mean in Trump's pronouncements? Does it mean to go to war with Mexico again, like we did in the 1840s, and take more of their land so that we can be a larger country? Does it mean going back to the past when religions were stronger and abortion was not possible? Does that mean going back to the 1950s and 1970s when laborers' earnings were a relatively large percentage of the CEO's earnings?

**"False attribution"** is the use by an arguer of unqualified or fabricated statements to back up his position. Trump did this when he cited a non-existent Muslim flare-up in Sweden to prove his anti-Muslim ideas. George W. Bush did this with his false accounts of John Kerry's lack of heroism in Vietnam. The Brexiteers did it when they asserted that the EU workers were using the healthcare system more than the British, so were tapping unjustly into the coffers of the UK. The truth was that European workers did not use the health service as much as the British did. They were also told that they could have the same deal with the EU that Norway had. But

Norway's deal cost almost as much per person as the UK paid and Norway was required to take in EU workers and migrants—the same conditions the Brexiteers wanted to eliminate.

Trump criticized CNN and MSNBC for "panicking markets." He said at a South Carolina rally — falsely — that "the Democrat policy of open borders" had brought the virus into the country. He lashed out at "Do Nothing Democrat comrades." He tweeted about "Cryin' Chuck Schumer," mocking Schumer for arguing that Trump should be more aggressive in fighting the virus. The next week, Trump would blame an Obama administration regulation for slowing the production of test kits. There was no truth to the charge.

Joe Biden, in a primary debate, said that Italy's single-payer insurance program was not handling the corona virus outbreak there. But Italy does not have a single payer insurance program. It has universal health care program financed primarily by a tax on corporations, supplemented by a sales tax—a VAT tax. Additionally, the average age of Italians who died was ten years older than Americans who died. Italy has one of the older populations in the world. In Italy 41% of deaths were to people over 80, and 35% were in the 70 to 80 year range.

Italy's health care system is ranked second best in the world by the World Health Organization. The U.S. is ranked 37th. Both countries were overwhelmed by the corona virus pandemic.

"A **false dilemma**" is presented when only two possibilities are given for a solution when there may be many possibilities. For example, saying that there are only two ways to deal with Islamic terrorism. Let them all in or keep them all out. In reality, there was already a very strong vetting process in place by the US government. So that is another option.

A few years ago in Norway, an Indian family was sent back to India because they were no longer in danger. The parents had responsible jobs, the daughter was in medical school and the son had the highest grades in his high school. Should India or Norway profit from the success of this family? Should the children be kept in Norway? Did Norway hurt itself in this action?

The fallacy of "**a single cause**" is another oversimplification of the facts in a very complicated world. Illegal Mexican immigration has brought in both hard-working contributing people and a criminal element. They did come illegally so can be returned, but what if they are contributing to the society? Is it the best option for America?

An "**incomplete comparison**" is a fallacy in which not enough information is given to make an accurate comparison. Trump continually said that he had "inherited a mess" but the truth was that: when he took over the unemployment level was under 5%, the lowest since the 70s, the stock market had gone up for seven years, most of the soldiers had been brought back from the Mideast, and President Obama was respected around the world as a peacemaker. Trump brought up no evidence for his claim.

Did Trump really have the best economy going with a growth of 2.1% in 2019. He told us that this was true, but it was not true! 2.1% should be compared with China's 6.0%, Pakistan's 3.3%, Philippines 6.2% Thailand's 2.4% Israel's 4.1%, Egypt's 5.6%, Peru's 3% and Saudi Arabia's 2.4%. In the unemployment area Trump's 3.6% was quite good. It equaled China's 3.6%, but it paled compared to Japan's 2.4%, Germany's 3.1%, Hong Kong's 3.1%, Singapore's 2.3%, and Israel's 3.4%.

So, before we believe, we should see the whole picture! A letter or a word is not the whole sentence, the whole paragraph, or the whole book. Of course, by mid-

March of 2020, the UCLA Anderson School of Business called the country in recession. But Trump had said three weeks earlier that the stock market looked good to him.

The corona virus had hastened the long overdue recession—and the American national debt was $3 trillion more in the hole with nothing to show for it. Then a few weeks later, because of the money borrowed to help the economy through the COVID-19 pandemic, it went to $5 trillion.

In March of 2020 Trump said that he had inherited an obsolete system for dealing with a pandemic. But in May of 2018, the top White House official, responsible for leading the U.S. response in the event of a deadly pandemic, left the administration, and the global health security team he oversaw was disbanded under a reorganization by National Security Adviser John Bolton. The abrupt departure of Rear Admiral Timothy Ziemer from the National Security Council meant that no senior administration official was now focused solely on global health security. Ziemer's departure, along with the breakup of his team, came at a time when many experts said the country was already unprepared for the increasing risks of a pandemic or bioterrorism attack. So who do you blame for the 22 month lack of an organization and administrator who were charged with preparing for a pandemic? Abe Lincoln was probably at fault. Certainly the "buck" never stops at Trump's desk!

The **"red herring"** fallacy occurs when the arguer does not answer the question but brings up another, often unrelated, situation and emphasizes that. Trump and his advisers do this continually. The press brings up the possible collusion with Russia in the election, and Trump answers that there were millions of illegal voters, or he answers that he supports Article 5 in the NATO agreement.

Still another type of fallacy is based on the idea that because it has been repeated so many times it must be true--**argument by repetition**. "Hillary is crooked." Trump said this 192 times that I counted. This was in addition to calling her a liar, corrupt, a fraud and incompetent. His basis for this seemed to be primarily her emails on a private server and the fact that she had made a great deal of money speaking-- often to Wall Street firms. The fact that he had made more money borrowing from Wall Street firms did not seem to be an issue, at least to him. But, of course, in politics as he saw it, there are no rules except to win.

This is a major problem in the process of electing representatives in many democratic republics. Repeat the lies about the faults or your opposition or your own accomplishments, usually with a controlled press, and your chances of winning are increased. Zimbabwe with Robert Mugabe, South Africa with Jacob Zuma, and Putin in Russia are just a few of the elected dictators around recently who have controlled the press. And they may be in the majority of national leaders. It is almost unbelievable that two of them are now gone because of the people's strong opposition to them. Venezuela's poor voted for a spreading of the wealth in 1998, but much of the educated part of the country left and the mismanagement by President Maduro left the citizens starving and ill.

The solutions to major problems are not as simple as politicians, or our limited knowledge, lead us to believe. In the 2500 years of democracies, some people have gained power by honestly proposing ideas that should improve the society. But there have certainly been large numbers of presidents and representatives who had lied to gain power and often maintained their power through the strong arms of the police and army. The ideal of "government of the people, by the people and for the people" is too often "government of the powerful, by the powerful and for the powerful." And, gaining that power is not always done ethically!

There can be overlaps in these fallacies in that something that is said violates more than one fallacy type.

"I believe in God, everybody does and nobody can disprove it." While God may well exist, the fact that the idea cannot be disproven or that everyone believes it, does not prove it.

## HOW TO FIND HOLES IN AN ARGUMENT

The third area of logic is the deductive. Here the argument is analyzed as to whether or not the conclusion follows from the two premises of the argument. It is possible to have a conclusion that is true even if the premises are false-- as long as the rules of deduction are followed.

While inductive logic looks at the possible or probable truth of a statement. Deductive logic looks at the structure of the argument to see if the conclusion follows from the premises.

When statements are put together to arrive at a more advanced level of knowing, this is called deductive logic. There are rules for arguments to be "valid." Deductive logic does not deal with truth as much as with whether or not the statements used in the argument follow the rules of sound thinking. The classic syllogism of deductive logic is:

All men are mortal.

Socrates was a man.

Therefore, Socrates was mortal.

The first two sentences are called the premises. The last sentence is called the conclusion. If it is true that all men are mortal, then the first premise is true. But not all people have died who have been born, so we don't know for sure that the first premise is true. But since all people who were born at least 200 years ago are now dead, it would appear to be true.

The second premise "Socrates was a man" is true if he actually existed. There is some historical basis for this fact.

There are several rules that must be followed for an argument to be valid. One such rule is that the term that appears in both premises (in this case it is man or men) must include all of the group in at least one premise. In this case, it is "all men."

When we look at the premises and the conclusion we have three terms: Man, Socrates and Mortal. When we are looking for relationships between these we must know just how much of each we are talking about. So we use modifiers which may not be in the premises or the conclusion. The modifiers are: all, some (one or more), or none. So the above syllogism would be:

> ➢ All men are (some of) mortals
> ➢ (All) Socrates was (some of) men
> ➢ Therefore (all of) Socrates was (some of) mortals.

But here is an example of an argument that is valid and the conclusion is true but the premises are not true.

> ➢ The moon is made of green cheese.
> ➢ All things made of green cheese are round.
> ➢ Therefore, the moon is round.

The conclusion is true but the premises are false. They don't pass the test of inductive logic. But, the rules of deductive logic have been followed.

The premises did not pass the standards of truth needed for an argument that might be used in seeking election. We might also look at the semantics of the premises. Which moon are we talking about? The moon of Earth, one of the moons of Saturn or some other moon? What do we mean by green cheese? And what do we mean by round? Do we mean a globe, a circle, something that is nearly a globe—like the Earth, which is really an oblate spheroid.

A similar syllogism from the Trump campaign might be:
- All businessmen can be effective American presidents.
- Donald Trump is a businessman.
- Therefore, Donald Trump can be an effective American president.

The argument is valid. The problems are with the premises. So it is an inductive problem. While this argument was not made in this form to the voting public, it was strongly inferred. And many Americans, not being aware of history, bought into it.

The problem with the first premise, as earlier noted, is that from the 1900s businessmen who became presidents have been ranked, on average, in the bottom third of presidents in terms of effectiveness: Hoover, Coolidge, George W. Bush and Harding are all at the bottom of the list of effective presidents. All were successful businessmen.

The second premise also has some problems. Donald Trump has not been a particularly effective businessman. His hotels and casinos have had four bankruptcies. His ownership of: a USFL football team, Trump Steaks, Trump Magazine, Trump Vodka, Trump Airlines, Trump Mortgage, Trump University, Trump's Travel Website-- all ended in failure. Add to that his many court cases in which he broke federal laws or contracts and we have some real doubts as to his business acumen and his ethics.

Just as in inductive logic, there can be fallacies when developing a deductive argument. You can have only three terms, or ideas, in a syllogism.
- Illegal immigrants are taking many jobs,
- I need more pay, so we should get rid of all immigrants.

Four terms: illegal immigrants, people who take jobs, I need more pay, getting rid of all immigrants.

Another is that you cannot have an affirmative conclusion from a negative premise:
- America is not doing well,
- Doing well requires a Trump election, so:
- Trump can make America great again.

There are several other deductive fallacies that can make an argument invalid. But this is not a logic class. These are only cited to make people aware of how we are often convinced of something even though it is not logical or true.

## BEWARE THE LOGICAL FALLACIES OF POLITICIANS

This book illustrates how modern-day politicians and capitalists may appeal to every aspect of our mind, from our unthinking and reacting unconscious mind, to our intellect. In the past in America, and today in Europe, it is the appeal to the intellect that politicians usually use. But recently, from George Bush to Brexit to Donald Trump we find an increasing use of irrational appeals to our unconscious minds.

Whether knowingly or unknowingly, politicians are using the psychological motivating insights that advertisers have used for decades. And, as will be shown, many politicians are hiring the same companies that advertisers use. If all is fair in love and war—no problem! But if it is important for you to know the truth before you step into the voting booth, or if it is important to have representatives that are educated and who are able to use the tools of logic-- we had better improve our education.

Two prominent Republicans: Mitch McConnell, the Senate majority leader (member of the Select Committee on Intelligence, and the Agriculture, Nutrition and Forestry Committee), and Marco Rubio, a major candidate for the presidency and (member of the Select Committee on Intelligence), both said recently said, relative to their denial of climate change, "I am not a scientist." They are also not women, can they legislate for them? They are not theologians, so can they believe in God?

The Florida Senator said that proposed policies to curb climate change "will do absolutely nothing" to improve the environment, but will "make America a harder place to create jobs." Since he is not a scientist, does he have any evidence for what he says? Or is it just uninformed wishful thinking— promulgated by lobbyists for the fossil fuel industry? There is absolutely no question that climate change exists. That humans have caused it, is affirmed by 98% of climate scientists.

Is it true that legislative policies "will do absolutely nothing?" Some 50 years ago it was found that the ozone layer, which filters out some of the ultraviolet rays of the sun, was decreasing. It was due, in large part, because of fluorohydrocarbons, from: refrigerants, like air conditioning units and refrigerators; propellants, like spray cans; and, some solvents. The increased ultraviolet rays were causing skin cancers and cataracts in humans, They also were damaging plants.

According to NASA, ultraviolet rays affect our DNA. This is true for both plants and animals. The United Nations estimated that a 1% decrease of the ozone layer resulted in a 2 to 3% increase in skin cancers. With plants, UV radiation interferes with photosynthesis in many species. Among them such crops as: rice, corn, soybeans, winter wheat and cotton.

By reducing the causative agents, the ozone layer is again increasing. It was scientists who discovered the problem and sounded the alarm. It was intelligent legislators that prohibited the manufacture of these culprits.

As serious as this was, it is nothing compared to the effects of climate change, which include: billions of dollars lost because of hurricanes, famines, excess rains, and higher oceans that can flood low-lying cities and farmland. These, of course, are just a few of the factors that result from our human meddling with our air and stratosphere.

With global warming, again it is scientists who discovered the problem and suggested the solutions. In much of the world, legislators have banded together to fight the problem. But this is a much larger problem than the ozone layer. At this time, all we can hope is that legislators will work to slow the damage being done. Perhaps we can speed the development of solar power, wind power, and electric cars. I wonder if Senators McConnell and Rubio have considered developing jobs in these areas. There is more to the industrial output of America than just coal mining!

Kentuckian McConnell also put jobs ahead of climate change and said, in his most scientifically verifiable theory that "I know lots of people who don't believe in climate change." This would be either an anecdotal fallacy, an argumentum ad populum (if some people think so, it must be true), or he is lying to us.

Do these legislators believe that the world is flat? It certainly looks flat—but I'm no scientist. Scientists found that it is almost round, an oblate spheroid—slightly flattened at the poles. If it were perfectly round we wouldn't have to fly the polar route from Europe to America! Do they believe in evolution? Biologists, anthropologists and geologists are certain it is true. Do these Senators ever fly on airplanes? Do they drive cars? Do they use computers? Scientists developed all of these technologies. I assume that the venerable Senators accept the technology developed by some scientists! Maybe they need to listen a bit more to what is empirically verifiable rather than what is politically expedient for some voters in Kentucky and Florida.



There have never been so many ways to deliver a true or false message. And there have never been so many ways to target specific audiences. In the past it was quite simple to target British citizens, or Catholics, or General Motors employees. Now you can target pro-life women in Woodland Hills, California, African-Americans in Chicago who are likely to vote, or people who may buy golf clubs in Dublin.

Facebook, Amazon and Google know as much about us as we do! Political, or other advertising, pitches are inescapable for people living in the electronic 21$^{st}$ Century. But is it possible to determine the fakes of the photo-shopped photos we see? Technicians can develop a video of Barack Obama telling us what a great job Donald Trump is doing, and how he was wrong; in advocating health-care for all, in opening relations with Cuba, or how he should have married Lady Gaga instead of Michelle!

The messages may be designed to encourage us to vote—or to discourage us. And, obviously, they go a long way in determining our choices. They even give us fake news on the corona virus. Recent fake news included: "drinking lots of water to wash the virus from the body" and "holding your breath for ten seconds to prove that you don't have the virus."

President Trump's digital operation has learned from some of the tactics pioneered by England's now defunct Cambridge Analytica, which was instrumental in influencing voters to vote to leave the European Union. Billionaires Trump and Brexit manipulator, Robert Mercer, used targeted messages in both elections to achieve capitalist goals. The EU regulations generally protected the citizens from those wanting to exploit them. The US had similar regulations. By exiting the EU, tough citizen-protecting laws no longer applied. By electing Donald Trump, the American regulations were torn up with great relish by The Donald.

How did the hedge-fund managers and others high in the capitalist hierarchy do it?

Direct marketing has been with us for 60 years, but only in the last few years has social media been available. There is so much information about us on Facebook, credit reporting agencies, and many other businesses that is sold to data brokers then resold to businesses and politicians. As an example, when I want to see a You Tube video, it starts with an ad for golf. I have recently looked up some prices on golf clubs for my wife on Google—I don't play anymore—but You Tube thinks I do!

That golf ad is not a problem. What is a major problem for modern elections, in most countries, is that Facebook, with nearly two billion monthly users is ideal. Its advertising revenue is in the multi-billion dollar range. Each global user is worth about $4 per year in revenue, and each American user is worth about $15 per year. Corporations and politicians are using both direct open advertising and "dark posts."

Dark posts may be targeted toward likely Trump voters such as "President Trump has appointed large numbers of pro-life judges. Make sure you vote on Tuesday to continue our fight." Or, they may be aimed at people whom the candidate wants to discourage from voting, like "Biden is a cinch to win our state by a million votes, so relax on Tuesday. Or, "Sanders wants to take away your personal doctor and replace him with an overcrowded clinic." Trump used such dark posts in the 2016 election. Politically interested people and parties throughout the world and on every shade of the political spectrum now use such targeted messaging.

Here is an example of a photo-shopped picture that is obviously untrue, so seeing is not believing anymore!

Just one big happy family—Barack, Hillary, The Donald and his buddy Kim, Vlad and Joe. I think this photo was taken at Hillary's Inauguration Ball! "Watch your hands, Donald!"

Modern technology can make videos of anybody saying anything. Here is a YouTube video of a University of Washington project faking a Barack Obama speech. If you are reading an e-book, just click the hyperlink, If reading the print version, write the address into the address bar.

https://www.youtube.com/watch?v=AnUC4m6w1wo

## IDENTIFYING AND TARGETING IDENTITY GROUPS

Bernie Sanders targeted the college students and those carrying student loans in both of his election attempts. Joe Biden targeted the anti-Trump moderates. Trump targeted the Evangelicals, both the Protestants and the Catholics, and business interests. Cigarette companies usually target people who feel inferior so they need the power of adulthood, and only adults can smoke.

Here are some identity groups that may be used in an election:
African Americans
Catholics
Pro abortion
Anti-abortion
Hispanics
Men over 50
Suburban women
College students
People who owe on their college loans
Evangelicals
College graduates

Here are some identity groups that might be used by an automobile manufacturer for advertising an electric car:

Environmental groups

College graduates

People who read more than 6 books a year

People in California

This may give you an idea of how propaganda, advertising or election messaging might be pinpointed. It might be more specific. For example, it might be African-American college graduates, who live in Chicago or Catholics who graduated from a Catholic University and are living in New York.

**FEW UNDERSTAND THE BASES OF OUR BELIEFS!**

There is so much on our minds today that few voters and legislators understand the basic facts relating to their opinions—or the basic assumptions that are fundamental to their belief system. Basic assumptions are fundamental, but often unprovable, assumptions that direct our thinking and behavior. This assumes that we are psychologically normal. We may or may not think our way into our values and our value-directed behavior. Many of our values are absorbed from our environments, rather than thought out through a careful analysis of our world and best way to navigate it. Parents, priests, pedagogues and playmates can be early sources of our values.

Other behavior is directed by our sub-conscious or unconscious drives and may have their roots in the malfunctioning of the brain or neurotransmitters or in our early experiencing of our world.

**PSYCHOLOGICAL SOURCES OF BEHAVIOR**

If a psychotic thinks he is Napoleon, his behavior will be largely influenced by his psychosis. If an agoraphobic (afraid to go outside) or aerophobia (fear of flying) acts different from you their behavior will be based on their phobias. Personality disorders, like narcissism, are relatively common. As we have seen from President Trump, they can have far-reaching effects from handling national problems, like the corona virus pandemic, to foreign relations, like thinking he could influence North Korea's nuclear ambitions.

Now we have another major problem in global politics. Whenever people with deeply entrenched psychic problems seize power, either by election or by other means, their politics can be directed by their unconscious mental states rather than by intelligent analysis and the logical projection of possible outcomes. Hitler, Napoleon, and Pope Urban II with his Crusades, come to mind.

Donald Trump's political directions often are manifestations of his lifelong inferiority complex which has long been exhibited as narcissistic and bullying traits. Political pundits attempt to analyze his tweets, programs, appointments and pronouncements as if they were well thought out ideas. This is often a major mistake. They may be American executive policy because of his lofty position, but they often derive from his unconscious mind, not from national or global realities and well-thought-out solutions to real problems.

Some of his ideas do come from his experience, like the concepts that business is more important than people, or that the rich should keep more of their money and should be able to pass it all along to their children. He is not alone in these beliefs. In fact, his major financial backers have the same primary concerns.

So it is a mistake to think that all of his policies emanate from the personality problems in his unconscious mind. But it is equally erroneous to believe that all of his agenda items have a well thought out and consistent orientation toward making America great again. Many of his ideas spring directly from his superiority complex and the ensuing bullying behavior. These, often contradictory ideas, however are masked by his rationalizations and lies. This combination of unconscious motivations, personal selfish ideas, his business-oriented views of the world, lack of experience in government, aversion to reading, aversion to advice by experienced people, and his impulse to win at any cost—make his "leadership" harmful to the U.S. and its allies. It makes it very difficult to find consistency in his policies and his nominations of the people whom he expects to carry out his ideas. The journalist or pundit must consistently change lenses from being a philosopher, to being a psychologist, to being a political scientist.

His erroneous views: of science, as seen in his rejection of the fact of climate change; his inconsistent ideas that outlawing abortion can be done while lowering taxes—because unwanted children must go to school (at an annual cost of about $10,000) and more often find their way to prison than wanted children; or that tax cuts can decrease the national debt--can readily be seen by most informed people.

On the other hand, he seemed quite presidential in his press conference in Singapore with Kim Jong Un. If what happened in the past is prologue, like Jong Un killing his half-brother, or his father's reneging on his agreement to stop his production of nuclear arms during the Clinton administration in 1994—he might be a little skeptical of his newfound friend. Has the North Korean tiger really changed its stripes permanently? If so, was it that Kim had encountered a bigger bully with a bigger red nuclear button? Was it the United Nations' heavy sanctions that had done it? Was it the pressure from China—it's biggest trading partner? Was is it just because he liked our Donald? Or was the real reason that he wanted a McDonald's in his capitol city? The facts are that we have two bullies who can change their minds faster than Superman can stop a speeding bullet. So, we'll just have to wait and see! The essential requirement is that there be no regime change in North Korea. Too bad for the North Korean citizens, but it does keep Kim out of prison and off the welfare rolls.

Most of Trump's predecessors, whether liberal or conservative, had relatively consistent sets of policies. They were generally easily understood—and might be relatively easily criticized using internal or external criteria. The problem with Trump's policies and programs, tweets and threats, actions and inactions are that we must seek different causes for what we see. Unconscious motivations, conscious selfishness, varied business or personal experiences, and campaign promises that were made off-the-cuff--have the pundits pondering their consistency. There is no consistency!

MENTAL PROBLEMS

The best people to evaluate mental health are usually the mental health professionals. Back in the days of the Cold War, Senator Barry Goldwater was a strong advocate of being tough on communism. The magazine Fact published a story titled, "The Unconscious of a Conservative: A Special Issue on the Mind of Barry Goldwater." (Fact magazine, 1964 (Vol. 1, Issue 5), was the source of the APA's Goldwater rule. Scribd has the full text at https://www.scribd.com/document/322479204/Fact-Magazine-Goldwater-1964)

In a survey of psychiatrists, 1,189 believed he was unfit to be president, while 657 believed that he was fit. 571 said that they didn't know enough about him to make an evaluation. Some of the evaluations were that his personality was paranoid, and akin to people like Hitler and Stalin. Other evaluations were more of a philosophical, rather than psychological, point of view. The liberal psychiatrists just didn't like him. Of those who supported him, he was called a realist. Others called the whole concept of the article as being asinine.

Goldwater sued the publisher of the magazine and was awarded $75,000, equivalent to about a half million dollars today. The Supreme Court refused to review the case. Because of the decision, the American Psychiatric Association decided that it was unethical to give a professional opinion about public figures that have not been examined in person. The so-called "Goldwater Rule," was adopted by that association, it states:

"On occasion psychiatrists are asked for an opinion about an individual who is in the light of public attention or who has disclosed information about himself/herself through public media. In such circumstances, a psychiatrist may share with the public his or her expertise about psychiatric issues in general. However, it is unethical for a psychiatrist to offer a professional opinion unless he or she has conducted an examination and has been granted proper authorization for such a statement."

There are several organizations of mental health therapists. The American Psychiatric Association (APA) is only one. The American Psychological Association (APA) is another. It also is concerned with protecting the individual being commented on. However, it does not seem to be quite as strict as the psychiatric association was. Another is the American Psychoanalytic Association (APsaA). It recently told its membership "that the responsible use of professional expertise in public affairs is permissible."

Varying mental health professionals have observed the behavior of Donald Trump and publicly stated that he has an assortment of personality problems, particularly: narcissism, a lack of empathy, and a superiority complex, or grandiosity. Some have said that he has a dangerous mental illness.

All known mental problems and illnesses are listed and explained in the "bible" of mental health therapists, the Diagnostic and Statistical Manual of Mental Disorders of the American Psychiatric Association. It is now in its fifth edition. (DSM 5 is the abbreviated title.) Under, "Narcissistic Personality Disorder" (Section 301.81) it is written that the narcissistic personality disorder (NPD) is becoming better known. There is not as much written about it as there is other personality disorders, but it is quite prevalent in the offices of therapists. . . These patients could not be classified as psychotic, and they were not typically neurotic, and were generally not responsive to conventional therapeutic treatment. It seems to be more common with males than females.

The symptoms are: grandiosity, seeking excessive admiration, and the lack of empathy. From the outside these patients act as if they are in control and are always right, and show condescending attitudes towards others. They cannot accept criticism. Even though some may achieve very high in some societal areas, they battle with strong feelings of low self-esteem and inadequacy.

Any five of these nine symptoms below is a strong indication of clinical narcissism. (American Psychiatric Association, 2013)

➤ Grandiose logic of self-importance
➤ A fixation with fantasies of infinite success, control, brilliance, beauty, or idyllic love
➤ A credence that he or she is extraordinary and exceptional and can only be understood by, or should connect with, other extraordinary or important people or institutions
➤ A desire for unwarranted admiration
➤ A sense of entitlement
➤ Interpersonally oppressive behavior

- No form of empathy
- Resentment of others or a conviction that others are resentful of him or her
- A display of egotistical and conceited behaviors or attitudes

Donald Trump seems to exhibit all of these symptoms. In the general population, we expect to see this personality problem in less than 1% of the cases. However, in the clinical settings of therapists, we find this in 2 to 16% of patients.

In a public statement Trump said "Actually, throughout my life, my two greatest assets have been mental stability and being, like, really smart." He also said that he "would qualify as not smart, but genius ... and a very stable genius at that!"

The psychiatrists who abide by the Goldwater rule, and lawyers, who are not mental health specialists ask how can therapists express a diagnostic opinion without ever having met him face-to-face in a therapy session? A well-known television personality, who is also a trial lawyer, has said that such diagnoses would never be allowed in a court of law.

Well, that trial attorney has not practiced diagnosing mental abnormalities. A face-to-face meeting or interpreting ink blots are not the only possible methods for making a diagnosis. A number of other options can give conclusive diagnoses. For example: Rorschach inkblots, word association and free association are often used as adjuncts to diagnosis. Paper and pencil answers to questions or drawing varying situations may also be used. But the best method of diagnosis is quite often merely observing the subject.

In family counseling, it is rather common to have the therapist watching from behind a one-way mirror to see how the family members interact with each other. It is well-known that when a person with sub-psychotic problems knows he is being evaluated for mental health, he is often sufficiently aware enough to give desirable answers to the questions of the therapist. This is quite different from a psychotic with a logic tight delusion. A patient who thinks he is Napoleon all the time will probably not hide this from the diagnosing therapist.

The Army's Field Manual on Leadership, lists the five crucial qualities of a leader: "trust, discipline and self-control, judgment and critical thinking, self-awareness, and empathy. Leaders must shape the objectives and ethical behavior of their followers. The core values of a leader include: loyalty, duty, respect, selfless service, honor, personal courage, and integrity."

Any objective evaluation of Donald Trump shows lying, a lack of self-control, huge gaps in critical thinking, selfish motivation, and a number of similar absences of leadership qualities.

But Donald Trump illustrates only one type of psychological factor that may affect our behavior—and the behavior of our leaders.

## VALUES AND BEHAVIOR

Another factor strongly influences our behavior—our values. All of us have values. We can see what they are by how we act. The saying that we must "walk the walk, not only talk the talk," illustrates this. The same observation is made repeatedly through history. "A person isn't what he says, he is what he does."

But why do we value what we value? When we examine why we hold a certain viewpoint, if we search for the foundation of our thinking we come to an unprovable assumption--a basic assumption. The three assumptions that all values can be traced to are: self-centered assumptions, God-based assumptions, and society-based assumptions.

Do we exist, does God exist, what is the best society—these are basic value questions.



As mentioned earlier, our behavior can be directed by unconscious motivations. These may be caused by biological factors such as the abnormal functioning of various parts of the brain or the neurotransmitters. There may also be genetic or epigenetic influences on our behavior—as they cause malfunctioning in the nervous system. Genetics refers to the influences of the genes on our behavior. Epigenetics refers to environmental factors, such as different stressors (ie. smoking, overeating, and psychological stresses) to oneself or to recent ancestors which have been passed onward through the sperm or ova. Environmental effects on an individual can begin during the embryonic state or at anytime later in life. These epigenetic changes affect how a gene will, or will not, work. For example, studies on the MAOA gene or epigenetic effects on various genes that affect one's impulse control, can overpower a person's value system regarding how to act during a stressful situation. But we will now put aside the psychological and concentrate on the logical.

Most of us agree that we exist. Although there was a religious philosopher, George Berkeley, who had the well thought out assumption that we are all ideas in the mind of God. We would therefore would not physically exist. There are not many who would accept his thinking today. So, most of us would believe that we exist as individuals. This is actually the major assumption used by people in expressing their values. Although they will often rationalize that their values are actually God-based or society-based.

Our individual values may come from our psychological needs or from logical fact- based decisions.

As examples of psychological drives influencing our value decisions, we might cite: the rising incidence of traffic deaths among low income countries where owning a car is a major source of power, and the faster one goes the more power one is exhibiting. With power being the major psychological drive, we see it:

- In bullying and abuse at nearly every age level.
- in the accumulation of money by professional athletes, media stars, and capitalist CEOs. Because what is a better indication of one's worth than a large bank account?

A "self" does not have to be an individual, it can be any group of people who have similar goals. It could be a family, a company, or even a nation.

Self-centered values predominate in the actions of most people.

- I believe in global warming but it won't make any difference if I drive to work.
- Donald Trump and his Treasury Secretary Steve Mnuchin downplayed the effect of the corona virus on the economy, saying it would pass quickly (their "self" was the U.S. economy). At the same time, investment banker Goldman Sachs was predicting a 5% drop the next quarter.
- To protect himself, Trump said that the whistleblower on the Ukraine phone call was wrong, but all the high-level testimony showed it was true.
- I'm going to buy a new car, because I deserve it.
- Come to my church, pray and contribute, and you will go to heaven.
- I am not happy in Turkey so I want to emigrate to Europe
- I am afraid for my life in El Salvador so I want to live in California
- I want free university education
- I want a minimum wage

➢I am poor and want children and I want the government to feed them

Advertisers and politicians commonly use the self-centered value reality to target their prey!

Two hundred years ago Alexis de Tocqueville observed that:

"Americans cleave to the things of this world as if assured that they will never die,… They clutch everything but hold nothing fast, and so lose grip as they hurry after some new delight. An American will build a house in which to pass his old age and sell it before the roof is on; he will plant a garden and rent it just as the trees are coming into bearing; he will clear a field and leave others to reap the harvest; he will take up a profession and leave it, settle in one place and soon go off elsewhere with his changing desires. If his private business allows him a moment's relaxation, he will plunge at once into the whirlpool of politics. Then, if at the end of a year, crammed with work, he has a little spare leisure, his restless curiosity goes with him traveling up and down the vast territories of the United States. Thus he will travel five hundred miles in a few days as a distraction from his happiness. Death steps in in the end and stops him before he has grown tired of this futile pursuit of that complete felicity which always escapes him. At first sight there is something astonishing in this spectacle of so many lucky men restless in the midst of abundance. But it is a spectacle as old as the world; all that is new is to see a whole people performing in it." (Book Two, Chapter XIII)

And later:

"In no other country in the world is the love of property keener or more alert than in the United States, and nowhere else does the majority display less inclination toward doctrines which in any way threaten the way property is owned." (Book Three, Chapter XXI)

And again:

"When an opinion has taken root in a democracy and established itself in the minds of the majority, it afterward persists by itself, needing no effort to maintain it since no one attacks it. Those who at first rejected it as false come in the end to adopt it as accepted, and even those who still at the bottom of their hearts oppose it keep their views to themselves, taking great care to avoid a dangerous and futile contest." (Book Three, Chapter XXI)

While self-centeredness, to some degree is expected of people, it seems to more prevalent in America at every level of society, and as de Tocqueville tells us, it has been present from our early years. This may be because the people who settled America were not content with their lives in England, Italy or China. They nurtured their self-interest with the accoutrements of wealth—as much as they could afford.

Self-centered values can be focused on the present or the future, the so-called delayed gratification. Do I want money for a car now? If so, working full-time at McDonalds may be the path to my value realization. But if my passion is to be an archeologist, a teacher or a veterinarian, I must plan on several years of college. My desire for an auto may have to be put on hold.

Most of us use self-centered values most of the time:
➢Shall I wear my red sweater or my blue sweater?
➢Shall I vote or play a video game?
➢Should I become a rabbi or an accountant?
➢Should I cheat on a test to pass the class?
➢Should I rob that man or go hungry?
➢Should I smoke a joint to relax?

We choose and act on our values continually. Even when we think we are using God-based or society-based values, they may actually be self-centered.

> I can go to heaven if I am "born again."
> Capitalism is the economic system I want because I own a major corporation.
> If I become a tele-evangelist, I can make a lot of money.
> If I pretend I am needy, society will support me.


Donald Trump has given us an excellent example of the nation as being a "self" in opposition to the "selfs" of the various states. With a more than $7 billion medical stockpile, Trump told the states that, "we're not an ordering clerk." The competition among state governments drove the prices for ventilators and protective equipment up markedly—by 300 to 500% with the national government sitting on a $7 billion stockpile,

Trump has insisted that it is not there simply to be deployed to states, but also for the federal government to use, adding states should have had their own reserves. Presidential son-in-law Jared Kushner told the press that it is "supposed to be our stockpile, it's not supposed to be states' stockpiles that they can use." Lt. Gen. Russel Honoré, who served as the Joint Taskforce commander during Hurricane Katrina responded, "The idea the stockpile is ours and the governors have got to have their own stockpile, is changing the narrative...That is bulls---and Jared Kushner doesn't know what he is talking about." Still, the Trump administration, after Kushner's comments, changed the website's description for the stockpile in order to downplay its use by the states. They removed the language saying that it was intended to be used by state, local, tribal and territorial responders who "request federal assistance."

The stockpile had been expanded under each previous president to include additional medical supplies and even the ability to set up a 250-bed hospital in a disaster zone.

During the H1N1 pandemic, the stockpile released a quarter of its inventory of antiviral drugs, personal protective equipment, and respiratory protection devices to help every state respond. The stockpile was also used to assist with the response to the Zica and Ebola cases in the U.S. Some vaccines, such as for smallpox or anthrax are only available in the stockpile.

Under the Trump administration, the management of the stockpile was moved out of CDC and into the Department of Health and Human Services, something former CDC Director Thomas Frieden warned at the start of the coronavirus pandemic could make it more difficult for resources to be quickly and effectively allocated. "There isn't an 'ours' or a 'theirs,' it's supposed to be considered as a single, centrally managed federal resource for rapid deployment to wherever it is needed," Frieden said.

Because of the Trump, disregard to the letter and spirit of the law, states have gone out on their own to get the supplies and equipment they need, it has created, according to New York governor Andrew Cuomo. a Wild West-style system with governors competing against one another and FEMA, driving up the price and having contracts canceled when a higher bidder comes along. While some states have received ventilators from the stockpile, New York was still short of the number needed and has continued to look elsewhere, Gov. Andrew Cuomo said last week. The state got 1,000 ventilators from China after the Chinese government facilitated a donation from billionaires Jack Ma and Joseph Tsai, the co-founders of the Chinese e-commerce giant Alibaba. The state of Oregon also volunteered to send 140 machines.

Yet Trump said that the U.S. still had about 10,000 ventilators and was in need of accurate information from the states about the number of ventilators and other supplies they have so the federal government could determine where to send resources.

On the other side of the Atlantic, in late March of 2020, Hungarian Prime Minister Viktor Orban secured the right to rule by decree after his Fidesz party passed a law in parliament granting him open-ended extra powers to fight the coronavirus outbreak. There was no ending date for his ruling by decree. This was not propaganda, but rather the power to control his government. This was similar, but more extensive, than Trump's tax break for the rich and for corporations in 2017.

## GOD-BASED VALUES

Depending on the type of supernatural that one believes in, the values may vary somewhat. For example, a pantheistic Hindu may place great emphasis on shedding certain desires from his mind so that he can be reincarnated at a higher level in his next life. A theist, such as we find in the Western religions, may believe in treating people well in this life so that he or she may gain paradise in the next life.

Often people assume that God agrees with their beliefs even if the Scriptures of their religion counter their beliefs. The approval of abortion in the Bible runs counter to the beliefs of many strong Christians who have not studied their religion's founding documents. (See below.)

Consequently, being "pro-life" gives one a feeling of power through the identity with others who are equally committed. So, when we express values that we think are religious values, we should understand their origins.

The truly devout believer lives values that he or she thinks their God really wants. But more commonly, people justify, often unknowingly, their self-centered behavior as being done for their God. Their behavior is most likely to be based on deep-seated psychological needs, like power. The 9/11 bombers or the typical ISIS member would be examples.

Of course, if you get the word directly from God, that is a commanding value. Hobby Lobby CEO David Green was refusing to close his arts and crafts stores during the COVID-19 pandemic because his wife, Barbara, received a message from God saying that the employees would be kept safe. Six years earlier, the corporation had won a 5-4 decision that allowed them to be relieved from a Dept. of Health and Human Services rule that required employers to cover the medical costs of contraceptives for their female employees because of the owner's religious beliefs. "As applied to closely held corporations, the regulations promulgated by the Department of Health and Human Services requiring employers to provide their female employees with no-cost access to contraception violate the Religious Freedom Restoration Act." (Burwell v Hobby Lobby (2014) 573 US. 682)

In another God-based value situation, some mega-churches conducted Sunday services when ordered not to by their governors during the COVID-19 pandemic. One Florida mega-pastor said that the church was an essential business, like markets and police. He also attacked the media for "religious bigotry and hate." The county and governor's orders required gatherings, including those held by faith-based groups, be fewer than 10 people to limit the spread of the corona virus. Many ministers ignored the society-based rules. As Rev. Howard-Browne said, "This is really about your voice. The voice of the body of Christ."

## SOCIETY-BASED VALUES

If we are actually society-based in some aspects of our lives, we need to understand the type of society we are advocating. The communists following the writings of Karl Marx, should understand the total theory of Marx's ideology, not just a feeling that people are equal and deserve equal treatment. The truly society-based values may be founded on equalitarian or libertarian principles or on some eclectic compromises between them.

Society-based values can also be the laws or regulations that the governing bodies decide on.

Donald Trump's value assumptions have been at odds with his advisors on many issues. As an example, during the COVID-19 pandemic, his assumption of what was best for the country, or his businesses, was the economy. His medical advisors were more concerned with slowing and stopping the number of disease cases and the number of deaths. He wanted massive loans for many affected businesses, even those who did not pay taxes. He wanted to ease the lock downs so that people would go back to work. The medical advisors wanted to extend the mandatory lock down, as China did.

China had required a complete lockdown of Wuhan and the surrounding areas in mid-January, after the first death was recorded. Within two months, there were no new cases in Wuhan. But a complete lockdown goes against the American values of freedom and the pursuit of money. On March 23, 2020, Trump proposed relaxing the lockdowns so that people can get back to work. This was on a day that had already seen 45,000 cases and 550 deaths. This was at a time when cases were doubling every day in New York City and in California.

While most countries followed the WHO guidelines, Sweden kept businesses open and did not quarantine. Their thinking, or lying, was that they wanted to get the whole population to be immune through an increased number of active cases. Neighboring Norway, on the other hand, followed strict quarantining and social distancing—thinking that immunity will come with a year when vaccinations become available.

With twice the population of Norway it had 59 deaths per million people (591 total deaths) from its 7,700 cases, with Norway having 16 deaths per million people (89 total) from its 5,900 cases. The "hero nation" among the Nordics was Finland with its 6 deaths from 2,300 cases. They were prepared because of their medical preparations and stockpiles from the Cold War.

## CONFLICTS IN VALUES

Conflicts in values are very common. The previously mentioned Hobby Lobby case pitted a woman's self-centered need for insurance-covered contraceptives and her agreement with the Federal government's society-based value regulation, against the God-based views of the business owner which was backed up, in this case, by the Constitution's freedom of religion guarantee.

The Supreme Court, as the lower courts, have ruled both ways when religious practices conflict with Federal or state laws. In Jacobson v. Massachusetts, 197 U.S. 11 (1905), a state, requiring a smallpox vaccination for all, was not an abridgement of liberty.

State courts have ruled both ways on whether or not Christian Scientists or Jehovah's Witnesses are protected in beliefs that run counter to medical knowledge. State required vaccinations, medically required blood transfusions, and other necessary medical procedures are examples. Most decisions are limited to state courts. They usually find that children are protected by the state. The thinking is that people have the right to believe anything they wish, but their practices may be limited. Adults are sometimes forced to undergo medical practices that they oppose on religious grounds. Children are usually required to undergo the medically recommended practices. One legal ground for requiring the medical procedure is that the state has a duty to protect its citizens.

In Gonzales v. O Centro Espirita Beneficente Uniao do Vegetal et al. 546 US 418 (2006) the religious group used hoasca, a drug listed in the Controlled Substances Act. It was allowed because the government had failed to "narrowly tailor" its prohibition of the drug. So religious (God-based) practices may be acceptable, even if contrary to Federal (society-based) law.

Another conflict can be seen in the U.S. government's aid to Israel. The U.S. was involved in the decision to form Israel. In spite of the fact that the per-person share of the national debt of Israel is about 25% less than the American per-person share, the God-based Judeo-Christian values of many Americans conflict with the self-centered values of some Americans to reduce governmental expenses. (So aid shouldn't be given to countries with less per capita debt than the U.S.) The society-based values may be on either side of the argument.. On the "pro" side, it is good to have a very strong army in the Middle East in case there are pro-Arab problems with America. On the "con" side, the Arab countries might align with the U.S. if Israel were not an ally of America.

In March of 2020, several governors reduced the size of permissible gatherings to reduce the spread of COVID-19. Some reduced it to 10, others to 500. The governors of Florida and Texas allowed churches to open, but the Governor of Louisiana set a limit of 10 in any group. Roy Moore, a candidate for the U.S. Senate, who was twice elected as the Chief Justice of the Alabama Supreme Court, and was twice removed for defying the order to remove a monument to the Ten Commandments that he had ordered placed in front of the court building. He was strongly against nationally guaranteed LGBT rights, but was accused of abusing under-age girls that he had dated in his 30s. He advised ministers to ignore the governor's orders on religious meeting limits based on the First Amendment right guaranteeing freedom of religion. In Mark 12:17 "Then Jesus said to them, 'Give back to Caesar what is Caesar's and to God what is God's.' And they were amazed at him." Is reacting to the corona virus a civic or religious responsibility? Certainly unleashing the virus was God's idea. Should governments try to fight it?

His continued advocacy of his view of God-based rights as superior to society-based rights might be rationalized by the possibility that if a worshiper died of COVID-19, he would probably go directly to heaven.

We often see the same conflict between God-based values and society-based values in the Supreme Court when five of the six Catholic-influenced judges generally select a religiously grounded argument, against a societal value, as seen in previous Court decisions or laws passed by the representatives of the people.

JUSTIFYING VALUE DECISIONS

People can arrive at their conclusions by psychological or logical means. In fact, all three value assumptions can be based on psychological needs or logical decisions based on the best evidence available.

> It's my country and I think that poor immigrants are bad for it;
> The country works better through meritocracy;
> We need a minimum wage;
> Everybody should have the opportunity for free college;
> We need a Nordic welfare system.

As the psychologist Alfred Adler observed, we all have inferiority complexes which originated in our infancy, when we: couldn't walk or talk, feed ourselves, or change our own diapers. We need power to overcome our inferiorities. We can use "power over" others to feel that power:

- My religious sect is the true one, yours is secondary;
- My gang membership makes me better than you;
- Have sex with me and I'll make you a movie star;
- You work for me, so do as I say;
- I'm your father, so do as I say;
- I have a new BMW;
- My family has always been Republican.

Successful people often find their power in the "power to" do things:

- My name is Gandhi and I led the demonstrations to free India from England;
- My name is Larry Page and with my friend, we invented the Google process;
- My name is Dwight Eisenhower, I was a successful general and president;
- My name is Coach Smith and I have helped many students to develop their potentials;
- My name is Salvador Dali and I am delighted with my art.

## LOGICAL EVIDENCE BASED GROUNDS FOR VALUE CHOICES

Using logic and factual evidence I might:

- Since I am overweight, I will wear vertical striped clothing to make me look thinner;
- Since I am overweight, I have undertaken a life-long reduction in calories and increased my aerobic exercise;
- I have read all the major scriptures for the world's great religions and I have decided to become a Buddhist'
- I had been pro-life based on my Catholic faith, but after studying my Bible I have become pro-choice.
- Looking at the happiness ratings internationally and our national debt, I think we ought to have some government ownership of some businesses;
- I'm for government provided health care, the societies that have it are rated happier in the United Nations' surveys.

So self-centered, God-based and society-based values can be developed based on sound knowledge and logic or on psychological needs.

Here are a couple of issues that have become important to many in the society, but have not always been studied beyond our opinions--which are not always based on evidence.

## ABORTION

Let's start with how so many don't have a grasp of what the Bible says relative to abortion. Still, several states have passed laws forbidding abortion and Donald Trump was elected President because he assured the evangelical Protestants and the conservative Catholics that he would appoint judges who would reverse the Roe vs Wade Supreme Court decision.  That decision was based on the liberty of the pregnant woman to make her own decision. The opponents of that decision want the liberty to have their convictions adopted by all.

The religious basis for the anti-abortion people is that life starts at conception, even though the Bible clearly states that it starts at birth.

Additionally, in Numbers 5:11, the Lord spoke to Moses about what should be the priest's duty when a woman has been accused of adultery. She is given "bitter water" to cause an abortion. In verses 21 and 22 it says when the priest is to put the woman under this curse—"may the LORD cause you to become a curse among your people when he makes your womb miscarry and your abdomen swell. May this water that brings a curse enter your body so that your abdomen swells or your womb miscarries." So, according to what God told Moses, abortion is required if a woman is pregnant from an adulterous relationship. In fact, it is part of the "curse" of her misdeed.

American laws that disallow abortions for rape, incest, and adultery would seem to be diametrically opposed to what God told Moses.

On the other hand, nowhere does the Bible say that it is not allowed in cases where it is voluntary. As Moses mentioned, there was at least one abortifacient that was known in those early times. Hosea (9:14) tells us that part of the punishment for not being faithful to the God of Israel is that "wombs that miscarry and breasts that are dry." So God will cause the spontaneous abortions.

THE FETUS IS NOT A PERSON—AND IS NOT SACRED

In Deuteronomy 28:18, God warns the Israelites that they must keep his Commandments. He cites the benefits of following them and the evils of disobedience. Among the evils are that: "The fruit of your womb will be cursed, and the crops of your land, and the calves of your herds and the lambs of your flocks.

Ripping open pregnant women is allowed by God for disobedience to Him, but it is also present in wars, which He could control if He so desired. God will punish the Israelites by destroying their unborn children, who will die at birth, or perish in the womb, or never even be conceived. (Hosea 9:10-16)

Even Jesus, in commenting on the approaching end of the world, thought not of sparing pregnant or nursing women. In Matthew 24:19 he said, "Woe to pregnant women and those who are nursing." So the often merciless God of the Old Testament may not be dead!

A FETUS IS NOT YET A PERSON—ONLY THE PROPERTY OF THE HUSBAND

EXODUS 21:22-25 "If people are fighting and hit a pregnant woman and she gives birth prematurely but there is no serious injury, the offender must be fined whatever the woman's husband demands and the court allows. But if there is serious injury, you are to take life for life, eye for eye, tooth for tooth, hand for hand, foot for foot, burn for burn, wound for wound, bruise for bruise."

GOD IS NOT PRO-LIFE

The killing of all people, including fetuses and children in Sodom and Gomorrah, is but one of about two dozen of such God caused mass extinctions. God certainly directed David's shot that killed Goliath. And in Jeremiah 44:7-8 it is said about worshipping other gods: "Now this is what the LORD God Almighty, the God of Israel, says: Why bring such great disaster on yourselves by cutting off from Judah the men and women, the children and infants, and so leave yourselves without a remnant? Why arouse my anger with what your hands have made . . ."

In 2 Samuel 11, we have the account of David seeing the beautiful Bathsheba, whom he had been told was married. He slept with her in an adulterous affair and she became pregnant. So David put her husband, Uriah, in the front of the ranks where he was certain to be killed—and he was. (Verses 14-17) Then Bathsheba became David's wife. So David was involved in an adulterous affair-- a capital crime. "If a man commits adultery with another man's wife—with the wife of his neighbor—both the adulterer and the adulteress are to be put to death." (Leviticus 20:10) It is echoed in Deuteronomy 22:22, "If a man is found sleeping with another man's wife, both the man who slept with her and the woman must die. You must purge the evil from Israel."

And it might be said that David planned the killing of Uriah. 2 Samuel 11:27, but that conspiracy is not clearly a Biblical sin, as it is in federal law where conspiracy to commit murder can bring up to life imprisonment.

Still, we are told that "the Lord was displeased with him." Perhaps it is like today where crimes by people in high places are not as severely punished as those committed by people farther down the pecking order!

SHOULD CHRISTIAN ADVOCATES SPEND MORE TIME ADVOCATING WHAT THE BIBLE HAS ACTUALLY APPROVED?

SLAVERY

One would expect that because of the Israelites enslavement in Egypt, that the message of the Bible would be totally anti-slavery. However, one finds strong pro- and anti-slavery positions in both the Old and the New testaments. A few of the many references follow:

Leviticus 25:44-46--"As for your male and female slaves whom you may have: you may buy male and female slaves from among the nations that are around you. You may also buy from among the strangers who sojourn with you and their clans that are with you, who have been born in your land, and they may be your property. You may bequeath them to your sons after you to inherit as a possession forever. You may make slaves of them, but over your brothers the people of Israel you shall not rule, one over another ruthlessly."

Exodus 21:20-21 --"If a man strikes his slave, male or female, with a rod and the slave dies under his hand, he shall be avenged. But if the slave survives a day or two, he is not to be avenged, for the slave is his money."

Exodus 21:26-27 --"When a man strikes the eye of his slave, male or female, and destroys it, he shall let the slave go free because of his eye. If he knocks out the tooth of his slave, male or female, he shall let the slave go free because of his tooth."

Exodus 21:2 --"When you buy a Hebrew slave, he shall serve six years, and in the seventh he shall go out free, for nothing."

And from the new Testament:

Colossians 4:1 --"Masters, treat your slaves justly and fairly, knowing that you also have a Master in heaven."

Ephesians 6:5 –"Slaves, obey your earthly masters with fear and trembling, with a sincere heart, as you would Christ,"

Titus 2:9-10 –"Slaves are to be submissive to their own masters in everything; they are to be well-pleasing, not argumentative, not pilfering, but showing all good faith, so that in everything they may adorn the doctrine of God our Savior."

1 Timothy 6:1-2 "Let all who are under a yoke as slaves regard their own masters as worthy of all honor, so that the name of God and the teaching may not be reviled. Those who have believing masters must not be disrespectful on the ground that they are brothers; rather they must serve all the better since those who benefit by their good service are believers and beloved. Teach and urge these things."

CAPITAL PUNISHMENT

The worst offense in the Bible is worshipping a false god. This is mentioned over 300 times and it carried the death penalty. Blasphemy is a similarly nasty offense. Adultery is sometimes a capital offense (Leviticus 20:10), as is murder (Leviticus 24:17) and sometimes rape.

Let us now move on to the next assumption that some people believe is the basis for the best society—or should we say, a "just" society. Should we look to the past, the present, or the future—and should we be violent, dishonest or rational in our advocacy?

# CHAPTER 5
## WHERE DO WE STAND ON THE POLITICAL SPECTRUM
## THERE'S MORE THAN JUST CONSERVATIVE AND LIBERAL.

What we think is "just" has a great deal to do with where we sit on the political spectrum.

Our old friend Aristotle thought that the rule of the mob, which he called democracy, was bad. But another form of rule, by intelligent and virtuous people, he thought was good. He called this "polity." We might call it an ethical and enlightened republic. Plato's version of the best government was to have philosopher-kings, who were the wisest, to rule. We might see it as the type of republic that we seek.

Some wonder if it is the mob or the intelligent and virtuous that elected Donald Trump, Robert Mugabe in Zimbabwe, George W. Bush, Jacob Zuma in South Africa, and voted for Brexit.

As we have moved through the book, semantics has been emphasized. We cannot think if we do not know exactly the meaning of the concepts with which we are dealing. If a Dane and an American are talking about how they agree on democracy, the Dane is probably thinking about the economic benefits of the welfare state and that they see the government's primary duty is to work for the happiness of the governed. The American is probably talking about the advantages of what he thinks of as capitalism and that it is the government's duty to keep taxes low.

## WHICH PATH?-- TO YOUR IDEA OF JUSTICE—OR OF HAPPINESS?

Objectively we can see that surveys indicate that Denmark is usually the happiest country in the world, never lower than third, while the US is about 16th to 18th every year. But the US is far lower in the amount of taxes paid--being at about 25%, the third lowest of the OECD countries, while Denmark tops them all at over 49%. Denmark ranks 13th in the world in terms of the quality of the infrastructure, while the US is ranked 25th.

What do you want--justice or happiness? Are they mutually exclusive? Is it fair that non-contributors reap the same benefits as the contributors to a society? Does having the 46 human chromosomes give you special rights? But what if the genes on those chromosomes are very, very different? Should that alter one's rights?

So, what has all this to do with democracy?

## THE POLITICAL SPECTRUM

The political spectrum was originally designed to label and differentiate between the different views we have of justice and what will make us happy. They are:

- ➢ Those who wanted to go back to the past, or what was thought of as the past—the reactionaries;
- ➢ Those who wanted to go slowly and conserve the values they had grown up with
--the conservatives;
- ➢ Those who wanted to move slowly in what they thought was the right direction--the moderates;
- ➢ Those who wanted to move more rapidly toward what they thought was the right direction, toward a social welfare state--the liberals;
- ➢ And those who wanted to move very quickly toward a welfare state, even using violence if necessary--the radicals.

We like to think that people have thought their way into their political views. In some cases, this may be true. But often, they have reacted into their positions based on their inferiority complexes and need for power and adopt a right wing view or because they have been loved effectively as children into a liberal position. We would hope that wherever one is on the five positions on the spectrum, it is based on: understood basic assumptions, sound semantic understandings, strong probable evidence, and sound logical reasoning. But such a hope is seldom a reality.

When people have arrived at a position because of their psychological makeup, their inferiority complexes and need for power or their ability to love unconditionally, they may rationalize their beliefs on the spectrum rather than having reached their positions thoughtfully through understanding their primary ideas and looking at the probability that their ideas may work.

My idea is to take the existing five elements of the political spectrum and limit them to rational opinions and sound logic. Each of the positions can be postulated by verifiable facts and potential projections. However, people often become so enamored by their beliefs that they may resort to psychological or physically violent means to obtain their desired ends. I therefore propose two additional categories on each end of the spectrum. The first addition to the spectrum would be propaganda, such as: fake news, lies, fake history and false promises. The farthest level on each end would be physical violence.

So the original five category spectrum might look something like this: **Radicals<Liberals<Moderates>Conservatives>Reactionaries**

Let's look at the traditional spectrum.

Starting from the far right, the reactionaries may want to go back to monarchy, to slavery, to irrational prejudices, to pure capitalism (in a Marxian sense), to what they believe to be a return to fundamental religion, to fascism, etc.

People typically call all those to the right of center "conservatives" and all those to the left of center "liberals." This is oversimplifying the possibilities and the range of beliefs. It would be like merely calling all Olympic champions or NFL quarterbacks athletes. Yes, they are athletes but there are a few major differences between a champion walker, a champion sprinter, a champion shot putter and a champion quarterback. Simplifying their prowess as merely "athletes" is equivalent to calling a king and a slave equally "images of God." We need to be more precise in our thinking.

I suggest that we use the traditional five categories and assume that they are logical and based on facts. For example, on the far right reactionary end, it is factual that people are not equal. No two people are exactly equal. They differ in age, height, weight, intelligence, knowledge, traditions, beliefs, work ethics, and family backgrounds. Should unequal people be given equal rights? Might this reactionary belief be then used to advocate serfdom or slavery? Might it be used to advocate monarchy? If we take an earlier idea of God, a vengeful God, an all-knowing and all-powerful God who is intimately involved in human affairs (and who gives to popes and kings the divine right to rule)—we have reactionary thinking.

## THE TRADITIONAL POLITICAL SPECTRUM

So on the extreme right we have the reactionaries who want to go back to a previous time, based on their religions or other traditions or because they profit by being the "haves." (People on the top of the economic, social, political and religious hierarchies have a lot to lose when the common people want equal rights or a larger share of the profits or decision making.) When we move from left to right, one of the major trends we see is a movement from equality to liberty (freedom)—and perhaps, inequality. Those who have the power and the money are already unequal monetarily to those who don't. Typically, they do not want to share either their power or their cash. They want the freedom to keep what they have.

Among the reactionary positions are: monarchy, fascism, neoliberalism, and alt-right ideologies like Neo-Nazism, and the KKK. The mythology of many religions is also reactionary in the age of science and the necessity to analyze any beliefs according to the probabilities that they are true—not just traditions. Unintelligent and uneducated people, or people who have not bothered to examine their traditional beliefs, are among those who lie in the reactionary safety net.

But there are other reasons to find oneself partially or totally in the reactionary area. This reactionary approach may be based on the fact that people are not equal. No two people in the world are equal to each other. To add a few more areas of inequality to the above list, we vary in: education, race, intelligence, religions, ethnicity, social status, industriousness, athletic ability, physical health, mental health, and a number of other factors. These differences may influence some people to want to return to an earlier time when some people were serfs or slaves or when women were chattels or otherwise inferior. They may want us to return to monarchy or to a time when national interests were settled by war.

Trump's plan to change Obamacare health insurance is to give tax credits for health insurance buying. The Tax Policy Center estimates that 45% of Americans pay no income tax—so would have no tax to subtract any tax credits from! Would they be able to afford insurance— especially if there were serious pre-conditions that might not be insurable? But they are not equal, so who cares?

Data from the British Election Study on the Brexit referendum shows that support for the reactionary position on the death penalty was a more reliable predictor of voting behavior than any standard demographic measure of age, income or social class. 56% of those over 60 voted to leave. We generally expect older people to be more reactionary and to want the "good old days." Being reactionary is not necessarily wrong. Even though liberals will use it as a derogatory term, oftentimes the past was really better. There are numerous reasons why the death penalty may be good or bad. (See: andgulliverreturns.info in Book 4 "On Human Values, in the chapter on the death penalty.). The death penalty can be good or bad from a self-centered point of view, a God based point of view, or a society-based point of view. It depends on your basic assumptions and on the evidence that you attach to those assumptions.

There are a number of factors that may influence a person to be somewhere on the spectrum. Family or social traditions, especially conservative religions, may put one on the right. Very often, positive experiences with other people of different social classes or different nations may put one more on the left. Quite often a strong belief in equal rights will put one more on the left. Being on the right is often more comfortable because of the traditions it protects. Liberty (freedom) is often found on the right especially when one inherits money, prestige or social standing.

Equality of opportunity is often advocated by people on both sides of the middle. However, the tools necessary for real opportunity are usually lacking. While the children of the richer parents may attend private schools, children in the ghettos and barrios may be in larger classes in schools, have less competent teachers, and fewer opportunities for supplementary education like foreign travel or computer summer camps. Additionally, teachers in the lower social class schools are much more likely to spend a great deal of time in disciplinary action because a major way for teenage children to achieve power in the lower social class setting is to disrupt the class.

Reactionaries might approve of any number of methods of execution: hanging, crucifixion, firing squads, electric chair, injection of poison—are all possible. But where the old traditions of violent executions used to exist, like hanging or the electric chair, in the US the liberal influence has made the death penalty less painful.

People on the right see people as unequal, usually with:

➢Unequal rights to life, if they are criminals (President Trump has proposed the death penalty for drug traffickers. Malaysia, China, Vietnam, Iran, Thailand, Thailand, Saudi Arabia, Singapore, and the Philippines already have such laws.);

➢Unequal right to health insurance if they can't pay for it;

➢Unequal need for eldercare if they have not paid into an insurance account;

➢Unequal right for a job if they have not prepared themselves educationally;

➢Unequal right to a top university if they cannot pay for it;

➢Unequal right to the top legal representation if they are poor and can only rely on public defenders; etc.

The feeling of equality on the left often includes the idea of Immanuel Kant and some religions that teach that every human life is precious no matter what the person has done. Consequently, a mass murderer like Anders Breivik in Norway has the same rights in Norway as any other person—well almost! Many of those people killed were or would become contributing members to the Norwegian society. This was certainly an economic negative for Norway because of the killing of its politically interested young people. Then the state had to tear down the government building Breivik had partially destroyed with a bomb. Then the state had to go to great expense to prosecute and defend him in the courts. Then they needed to hire extra guards to make sure he wouldn't kill himself in his three-room prison cell. Then a few years later he again went to court against the state, with the state paying the expenses, while he contended that he was treated inhumanely because he could not talk to other prisoners. At the lower court level, he won because everyone has equally valuable human rights, according to the European Union's granting of rights.

"The prohibition of inhuman and degrading treatment represents a fundamental value in a democratic society. This applies no matter what — also in the treatment of terrorists and killers," wrote judge Helen Andenaes Sekulic in her ruling. The ruling also said that the Norwegian state had not violated Breivik's right to a private and family life.

While just being "human" gave Breivik many rights, in spite of his lack of any showing of responsibility, under the European Union's Convention on Human Rights, The UN Declaration of Human Rights requires some responsibilities toward others in the society. After 28 articles granting rights, Article 29 states:

1. Everyone has duties to the community in which alone the free and full development of his personality is possible.

2. In the exercise of his rights and freedoms, everyone shall be subject only to such limitations as are determined by law solely for the purpose of securing due recognition and respect for the rights and freedoms of others and of meeting the just requirements of morality, public order and the general welfare in a democratic society.

3. These rights and freedoms may in no case be exercised contrary to the purposes and principles of the United Nations.

Equality, usually enunciated as equal rights, has emerged as superior to liberty in many instances in Europe. What they do not seem to acknowledge is that equality of opportunity is often denied to worthy people because so much money is being spent to enforce equal rights for antisocial people. If we take the millions of dollars that are being spent on Breivik, we wonder if it could be better spent in Norwegian schools and colleges. And if they don't need the money might it be better spent in education for deserving people in Africa, India, Afghanistan, or even Scotland?

## PEOPLE MOVE FROM ONE CATEGORY TO ANOTHER—BASED ON THE ISSUE

It is obvious that many people will flip back and forth between liberal, moderate, and conservative on different issues. For example, they may be for capital punishment, which puts them on the right, and for free college education, which would put them on the left. Quite commonly in the UK and Norway the conservative or reactionary idea of monarchy is cherished while a liberal welfare state is equally loved.

A person may be against the wearing any religious symbolism such as: a hijab or burqa, a cross, or a yarmulke—which would put them on the far left but also deny climate change which would put them on the far right, in the "reactionary" category. They may be for free public education, which would be a liberal position, but also for school vouchers, which would be a conservative position. They may be willing to take up arms to fight communism any place in the world, a far-right position, and also willing to go to war against oppressive dictators in the Middle East, a far-left position.

**The reactionaries,** as mentioned, want to go back to a real or imagined past. They may also deny science, since it rattles our modern minds with possibilities we could never imagine. Science is often not emotionally comfortable.

**The conservatives** tend to want to keep the values of their religious upbringing and other traditions. This gave the churches more power. China and Russia eliminated the churches, now they have returned. In France and the U.S., they had to be content with marginalizing the churches. But with liberty came a number of freedoms, including freedom of religion, that gave the churches a foothold.

As we have cautioned throughout the book we must understand the meaning of a term. For example, we often hear the term "neoliberalism" and may mistakenly believe that it is a position on the left, a new kind of equalitarian thinking. Actually, it is generally used in a reactionary sense meaning: privatization, deregulation, fiscal austerity and the 19th century capitalist ideas that pre-dated the welfare state and other liberal ideas.

Other social changes, such as gender identification and vocational possibilities in the digital age, are difficult or impossible to live with. How can people have sex with people of the same gender? Marriage can only be between a man and a woman, like mine is. When I go to the market, I want a human checker—not a robot scanning my groceries.

**The moderates** recognize that the world and society are changing and we must keep up with the changes. For example, climate change is a reality. There are genetic, epigenetic, and environmental influences that can influence our gender identities. The moderates recognize the need to preserve the world, but that it is changing. Information technology and robotics are factors that significantly change the way that employment in developed countries will evolve. Services, rather than manufacturing, are essential in developed countries.

**Liberals** are more likely to want to move faster than the moderates in anticipating changes. They usually are interested in developing more equality in the society. They tend to be against kings. The Magna Carta was such an equalitarian exercise. It was really between nobles and the king—but at least it took some of the power from the top and spread it around to others near the top—like the freemen. But 90% of the population, the serfs, were not included. However, during the last 800 years, more equal rights have seeped to the bottom of English society, still much of the land is owned by royalty. But why not? God gave the land to the kings and nobles in Medieval days—and God does not go back on His word. But wait a minute! What makes us believe in a God? Why should people inherit anything, titles or wealth, when they didn't earn it? We should all start as close to the same starting line as possible. And if some of us lag behind the average we need to give them a helping hand. The homeless, the drug dependent, the prisoners, and the otherwise needy must have our help.

**The radicals** want change faster. They might use violence to achieve their ends. The leaders of the revolutions in America, France, Russia, and China are prime examples of radicals who wanted to replace the traditional leaders of the society with a more democratic government of the people. But there are always leaders who want their ideas followed—and maybe everybody wants power! In Russia and China, it was concentrated in the Communist Party. In America and France, the idea was to get more liberty to those who could wield it.

BUT FIRST—A LOOK AT THE PSYCHOLOGICAL SPECTRUM

Another continuum that is somewhat akin to the political spectrum is the psychological spectrum of selfishness to the ability to love humanity. There is a similarity in this spectrum to where a person, or a society, sits politically and psychologically.

Here the continuum would be read from right to left.

**HUMANITARIAN << ABILITY TO LOVE A FEW<< SELFISHNESS/ LOVE                                                        NEED FOR POWER**

Infants are totally self-centered. Their only concerns are: being fed, changed, played with, and cuddled. If they are cuddled enough they may be on their way to what Erich Fromm called the stage of self-love, which might come somewhere after age four.  In this stage they realize that others are also important, so selfishness dwindles somewhat.  Eventually, according to Fromm, we might be able to develop the general ability to love—and the highest form of that is humanitarian love. Not many reach this stage.

As a nation, the U.S. tends to be on the selfish end of the spectrum. The concerns are for making money and saving on taxes, while demanding things like Social Security and Medicare that we only minimally finance. So, let the government borrow from Japan and let our children pay back the loans. This is not to say that there are not people who are individually humanitarian. We see that when there are tragedies that require charity—with many Americans giving both money and time.

Nationally, on the other end of the psychological spectrum, we could see the Scandinavian countries where they are much more equalitarian and are quite willing to pay high taxes for the good of the general welfare. The national consciences of the Scandinavians tend to be very liberal—and loving.

The political spectrum can often, but not always, be seen as the societal applications of the psychological continuum of selfishness to love. Here are two recent situations in which the three types of ethical, or value, assumptions can be seen where they are complicated by the empathetic attitude of humanitarian love. Then let's throw in some intellectual questions to complicate the matter.

Let us briefly look at two recent situations. People from Honduras were escaping the high murder rate of their country. They traveled across Mexico with the idea of finding refuge in the United States. At the border, the adults were arrested and the children were taken from the adults-- because they were not allowed to be taken to prison. Priests and ministers, using the passages of the Bible that require charity, frequented the media outlets.

Here we have the self-centered desires of the potential immigrants played against the society-based values, presidential regulations, and laws of the United States. But the outcry of the cruelty of taking children from their parents was deafening. The Attorney General cited the Bible, where St. Paul tells the Christians in Rome to obey Roman law. So, we have the three basic assumptions of ethics used in this battle.

In a parallel situation in Europe, migrants from a number of countries in the Mideast and southern Africa attempted to land in Italy. They were turned back and allowed to land in Spain. Italy has huge economic problems and has already taken in more than 100,000 migrants in a recent year. Their newly elected government was elected largely to control and even reverse immigration. Again, we see the self-centered desires of the migrants in conflict with the needs and laws of the society. The God-based ethical assumptions were not much of a factor in this situation.

So we have a group of people who are not highly educated, often of a different religion, nearly always from traditions that are different from the countries they want to accept them. The ethical and legal assumptions are clear that they have no rights. BUT, our psychological propensities for empathy often cloud the legal aspects. We see crying children. We see mothers nursing their infants. What human being cannot feel sorry for them?

But are the non-accepting countries ultimately to blame? Should the refugee parents have brought children into such a terrible world? Should the governments of the emigrants have protected all of their citizens? Should the government have enacted laws that would have protected babies from being born into such a lawless or non-economically fertile environment? In Honduras should the president have followed the idea of President Duterte of the Philippines and had police and vigilantes shoot the violent gang members without a trial? Should the ideals of a government of the laws and of fair trials be seen as superior to a society that might live in peace and prosperity? Yes, we have the assumptions of the far, far, far right against the assumptions of the liberal left.

And who said that ruling would be easy?

Now let us look at the expanded political spectrum.

A WIDER SPECTRUM

It seems to me that the political spectrum that we commonly use is too limited for a complete description of the possibilities of politics or belief systems. I propose a nine-category spectrum.

We will assume that the middle five of the traditional categories are nonviolent and logical, based on facts as well as on preferences. The categories, from right to left are:

1. Violent Reactionaries
2. Reactionaries who lie and use propaganda to achieve their goals
3. Honest thoughtful reactionaries

4. Conservatives

5. Moderates

6. Liberals

7. Radicals who want change faster

8. Radicals who lie and use propaganda to achieve their goals

9. Violent radicals

These can be laid as a continuum 9< 8 <7< 6< **5**> 4> 3 >2 >1

## WE SHOULD BE ABLE TO TALK TO EACH OTHER

The various categories along the spectrum may contain adherents who fell into their beliefs by tradition or by listening to others. They may also contain adherents who climbed into their beliefs by thinking, researching, and discussing. So far, no one has all the answers to all the problems facing our world.

In May 2017, Vice President Pence was giving the commencement address at the University of Notre Dame. About a hundred graduates got up and walked out. Why? Was it because he had left the Catholic Church to become an evangelical, since he calls himself "an evangelical Catholic." Was it because of his opposition to abortion? But this is the same position that the Catholic Church takes. Was it because he was a reactionary and they were liberals? But might they have learned something from him? Were they afraid that their minds, which they had made up before or during their university experience, might be changed?

It is often said that we should not argue about politics or religion. This is because every religious point of view and every political point of view usually rests, at least in part, on basic assumptions that cannot be proven.

How can you prove there is a God or heaven? How can you prove that people are equal or unequal? How can you prove whether liberty or equality is the more important basis for our government?

But there are other areas in religion or government that may be provable.

➢ Do Mormons break fewer laws than other religious people or nonreligious people? Here we could just look at the percentage of prison inmates of the various religions and the nonreligious.

➢ Does climate change really exist? Here we can look at: the measured temperatures over the last hundred years in over a thousand worldwide temperature stations; the temperatures from the last 2,000 years as shown in coring research in the oceans or in Antarctica; the number of major hurricanes, rainstorms, and snowstorms over the last 50 years.

➢ Can we find jobs for the huge number of unemployed young people? Here we can look at the incredible increase in population and the various types of technology that do the work that humans used to do

➢ Are there more or fewer advantages to capital punishment for a modern society?

So here are the categories for the expanded nine category political spectrum. Where do you fit on this political spectrum? And do different issues have you in different categories? What about: capital punishment, minimum wage laws, the use of DNA links to identify criminals, equality between men and women, euthanasia, abortion, data mining for electioneering?

## VIOLENT REACTIONARY ACTIONS-- THE FAR-FAR-FAR RIGHT

Moving back to a supposedly earlier time, whether real or imaginary, is a great political technique. When it involves killing as its political technique, it delivers a forceful message from its often-cowardly messengers.

Hitler called for the extermination of Jews and other undesirables in order to bring Germany back to its pre-Depression state. The alt-right's pro-Confederacy march in Charlottesville, Virginia in August of 2017, the Ku Klux Klan's violent actions, the shootings of abortion-performing doctors, Dylann Roof's shooting of nine black churchgoers, and Canadian Alexandre Bissonnette's murdering of 6 praying Muslims in Quebec—are examples of this belief. Perhaps the most violent individual action in this regard was done by the aforementioned Norwegian neo-Nazi Anders Breivik in 2011 when he killed 77 people and injured hundreds through his bomb and his automatic weapons. He didn't like the left-leaning government of his country. Recently a group of Bulgarian vigilantes, both men and women, has been hunting immigrants and refugees with the purpose of killing them. Then there are: the anti-Mexican shooting in El Paso that killed 22 and the anti-Muslim, anti-Black and anti-Jewish shootings. Germany has seen a number of violent actions, as have other countries in Europe and South America,

The terror of Al Qaeda, ISIS, and the many allied groups is a major reactionary goal. Going back to setting up a caliphate from Europe to Asia, and possibly for the whole world, is reactionary. A thousand years ago such a caliphate existed from Spain, across North Africa, up to Turkey, and across the Mideast and India. These were the glory days of a dominant intellectual Muslim conquest. Seeking to return to this, and an even more extensive caliphate, is the stated goal of many Muslim terrorists. Calling them "radical Islamic terrorists," is actually not semantically correct They are not seeking a new and equalitarian caliphate, they should be called "reactionary Islamic terrorists," because they are trying to go back to what once was—or what they imagined once was.

The President of the Philippines, Rodrigo Duterte, has given the police orders to kill drug suppliers and he brags that he has done such killings himself. When the corona virus hit the Philippines and he gave orders for everyone to stay inside, he OKed shooting violators.

The killing of former Russian spies in England recently is such a violent reactionary act—if they were ordered by the Kremlin, as is generally believed in the West.

In Dylann Roof's killing of the nine black people praying in 2016, we always wonder if his animosity toward blacks and his thought that a race-war was coming was psychotic, merely an illustration of a severe inferiority complex, or whether he really thought his way into this irrational behavior. As we have repeatedly indicated, it is common for people to believe what a person says or does without searching for the underlying subconscious motivations.

A report that tracks white nationalism, white supremacy and hate groups, identified 155 white nationalist groups in the U.S. in 2019, up from 148 in 2018 and a 55 percent increase since 2017.

Authorities say the gunman in the El Paso shootings told police that his target was "Mexicans" and that he posted a manifesto before the attack that included anti-Latino and anti-immigrant rhetoric. The gunman's manifesto contained white nationalist talking points on "ethnic displacement" and "race mixing" and refers to immigrants to the United States as "invaders." He obviously was ignorant of the fact that Texas was taken from the Native Americans by the Spanish. Mexico was formed and in the early 1800s Americans were allowed to settle there. In the mid-1800s the American president, James Polk, wanted more of Mexico's land and won the war that made it American. Polk strongly advocated expanding the boundaries of the U.S. and bringing Protestant Christianity to the backward Catholics to the south. The war cost $100 million and nearly 2,000 dead soldiers.

He did, generously, give Mexico $15 million for California, Arizona, New Mexico, Nevada, Utah and parts of Wyoming and Colorado. The Mexicans really snookered Uncle Sam on that one!

## RADICAL RIGHT'S FEAR OF "WHITE GENOCIDE"

The most powerful force animating today's radical right—and stoking the violent backlash—is a deep fear of demographic change, and the idea that "white genocide" is under way.

That ideology is believed to have been followed by the gunman in the attacks on two mosques in Christchurch, New Zealand, on March 15, 2019. White nationalist violence is also rising globally.

As the country continues to experience white nationalistic terror, extremist ideas long believed outside of the realm of legitimate politics are finding their way into the mainstream, in reactionary public policies that target immigrants, LGBTQ people and Muslims.

Inclusive democracy is the target of hate and bigotry. White nationalists no longer seek to simply spread their views — they are committed to seizing the power of the state.

It is not only non-white groups that are targeted, anti-LGBTQ groups are increasing.

The FBI found last year that nearly 1 in 5 crimes were motivated by anti-LGBTQ bias. But the Bible (Genesis 1:31) says that after God created the world "God saw that all he had made, and it was very good." But then, spending your time on hating and practicing violence, doesn't leave a lot of time for reading or clarifying the bases of what you say are your beliefs.

There is always a question as to whether some of these violent people were psychotic and using reactionary thinking to stimulate their irrational behavior or whether they had really thought their way into their killings. And if so, exactly what positive results did they expect would emerge from their murderous behaviors?


## LEGAL REACTIONARY PROGRAMS

In Singapore, possession of 15 grams of heroin is a capital offense—and you can expect to be hanged if you violate this law. While the number of hangings has decreased, recently two immigrants were hanged under this law. Malaysia and Indonesia have similar laws. In the Philippines, after President Duterte's 2016 ordered executions of drug dealers and drug users, over 6,000 suspected drug users have been executed without trials. (Trials are more likely to be held when governments are moderate or liberal.)

Such violence, in law enforcement, is more common in Asia than in the West, where individual lives are held to be sacred and where individual desires are often excused even when they disrupt an orderly society. In Asia, the society as a whole, is more likely to be the overriding concern.

In the U.S., funds spent on the drug problems take money from other valuable societal duties such as paying for education through the graduate level of the universities. There is only so much money to run a society. Singapore's home minister, when asked why his country used such forceful methods to curb drug use said, "show us a better model, a model that is as effective in reducing drug use." Some U.S. states have gone the other direction—taking the radical route of recognizing individual desires as rights and hoping to reduce criminality by legalizing some drugs, and giving heroin addicts methadone or free needles.

This is, indeed, a question for modern society. Should individual desires that are counter-productive for a society be allowed because of a notion of "human rights," or should the rights of others in the society, who are not drug dependent, be at least as important as those of the addict or the habituated person? Should society's money be spent to attempt to rehabilitate the drug addict or should it be used to fund the college education of someone who has avoided the lure of chemical happiness and who might be an important contributor to the society?

Another action that may be viewed as unjust is the imprisonment of suspected terrorists. The US has imprisoned a number of men whom they call dangerous terrorists. They are quite certain of their evaluations but do not have enough evidence to bring them to trial. So, the speedy trial promised by the Constitution does not apply to these non-citizens who are suspected terrorists, during what the government calls "a time of war." China recently jailed, beat, and killed a human rights advocate who worked in a high position in the government. In Turkey, after the failed coup attempt, thousands were jailed on suspicion of being sympathizers. Imprisoning such foes has a long history for both reactionaries and radicals.

Assassinations are almost the rule rather than the exceptions in our political worlds. They go back at least to the 11th century BCE in Egypt with the assassination of Ramses III, to the third century BCE in Rome, and to the seventh century in Greece. Known assassinations reach into the hundreds throughout the world. They are perpetrated by both far right and far left murderers. In the US, the assassination of President Abraham Lincoln is a prime example of the far-far-far right's determination for a return to the past.

Dictators must continually eliminate, either verbally or physically, those who oppose them. The Chinese Constitution makes this legal. While many basic freedoms are guaranteed by their constitution, such as freedom of speech and freedom of the press, citizens must realize the sovereignty of the state in exercising these freedoms, as shown by these elements:

Article 51.

The exercise by citizens of the People's Republic of China of their freedoms and rights may not infringe upon the interests of the state, of society and of the collective, or upon the lawful freedoms and rights of other citizens.

Article 52.

It is the duty of citizens of the People's Republic of China to safeguard the unity of the country and the unity of all its nationalities.

Article 53.

Citizens of the People's Republic of China must abide by the Constitution and the law, keep state secrets, protect public property and observe labor discipline and public order and respect social ethics.

An official at the Israeli Embassy, in January of 2017, was caught saying that the members of Parliament in England who opposed Israel should be "taken down." When it was revealed what he had said, he was released from his embassy job and his remarks were countered by official statements from the embassy. But it should come as no surprise that the Israelis, as many other countries, use lethal and other techniques to silence their critics.

Fascists commonly use both violence and propaganda to gain their power. As you remember from our discussion of semantics, fascism was defined and expanded in the essay titled, "The Doctrine of Fascism" by Giovanni Gentile in 1935. Benito Mussolini added a bit to the end of the essay. Gentile rejected democracy, liberalism, and Marxism. People are not equal, so they should not have an equal say in governing. In fact, the state is primary. Mussolini told us that you gain power by plucking the chicken one feather at a time. Pluck too fast, and the people will know what you are doing. Toward the end of his career he plucked too fast and the people skewered him and hung him upside down in a square in Milan—sort of a *pollo alla Milanese*!

## THE REACTIONARY PROPAGANDISTS—THE FAR-FAR RIGHT

This is the major topic of this book. As illustrated. it was used by George W. Bush in his campaigns, particularly when trying to minimize John Kerry's heroism in Vietnam.

It was used to a greater extent by the Brexiteers, and was probably used more than anyone else in history by Donald Trump in his primary and presidential quests and in his presidency. Fake news, fake history, and alternative facts were the overwhelming rhetoric. Russia seems to be involved in this area now in both the American and the German elections, as it was in Brexit and in the Trump campaign.

But this falsification of facts is not new. Backers of Thomas Jefferson called John Adams an hermaphrodite in their presidential contest. Joseph Goebbels was the Minister of Propaganda for the Nazis during World War II. Tokyo Rose used her wily ways to try to influence American soldiers in the Pacific Theater to be concerned about the unfaithfulness of their wives and girlfriends back home, and that they should stop attacking the Japanese.

Fox News, often called Fox Views, is a television station that often slants the news far to the right. It is one thing to report selected news and to offer propaganda to back up an anti-liberal viewpoint. It is quite another to fabricate news events. In 2009 the Sean Hannity program misrepresented video footage purportedly showing large crowds on a health-care protest orchestrated by Representative Michele Bachmann. Jon Stewart, of the Daily Show, showed inconsistencies in the backgrounds of the videos and revealed that the crowd shots were actually of a Glenn Beck rally some time earlier. This was not an isolated case. One might wonder if freedom to speak falsehoods should be allowed on news programs. So far, the Supreme Court has not objected. But European nations are not so inclined!

Trump violated the rules of formal logic hundreds of times in his Democratic Primary advance and hundreds of times more in his presidential quest versus Hillary Clinton. He was aided by far-far-right wing radio, television and newspaper commentators. In her recent book, Hillary talked about the unnerving technique that Trump used during the second debate. He would follow her around the stage in close proximity, making faces while she was trying to make legitimate points. His uncouth antics made the audience focus on him, as a superior man toying with a woman. It was a non-verbal propaganda message.

He continued to use such techniques to convince the American people, particularly his base voters, that the previous administration had used illegal wiretaps against him. There was no evidence that this had ever happened and the director of the FBI and others said that his charge was untrue.

Another example of propaganda is the Trump denial of climate change because it is bad for the fossil fuel industries—and some of his major contributors. This has resulted in government agencies having to use the term "weather extremes" instead of "climate change." They have also been told to use the term "resilience to weather extremes" rather than "climate change adaptation." Other meaningless phrases have been inserted in place of terms like "sequester carbon" and "reduce greenhouse gases."

Then there was the infamous Nunes memo that was declassified by President Trump and publicized worldwide. The four-page memo was an abridgment of about 100 pages of secret testimony before the House of Representatives Intelligence Committee. The Nunes staff members who compiled the memo eliminated essential information that would have been a more complete picture of what happened in this very small chunk of testimony before the committee. The memo was opposed by all of the Democrats and some of the Republicans but was deemed essential to show the political motivations of the investigation into the possible involvement of the Russians in the 2016 presidential election. The memo was originally classified, but was declassified by President Trump and released to the media.

There is an old saying that "a text taken from its context is a pretext." A pretext, of course, is a ruse or ploy that is removed from truth. For those who believe in the Bible, they should understand that the Bible says, "there is no God." That is a very powerful text. But if we look at the full context, the full verse says, "The fool says in his heart, 'There is no God.' They are corrupt, they do abominable deeds; there is none who does good." (Psalm 14:1)

Objective analysis might consider such a political technique, of using a pretext to be an objective truth, to be a "corrupt and abominable deed."

In early 2018, a huge outcry erupted from many Republicans, or right leaning public servants, such as: former FBI director James Comey, present FBI director and Trump appointee Christopher Wray, Rob Rosenstein of the Department of Justice who is ultimately in charge of the investigation, Robert Mueller, who is conducting the investigation, and former presidential candidate and Senator, John McCain. They believed that the declassification and release of the memo was counter to the interests of the American people by revealing sources of intelligence.

Such a release for political purposes might very well inhibit future informants from aiding in American intelligence gathering. The Democrats concurred with this breach of confidential intelligence gathering and added that the report was incomplete, having edited out essential information. This made it a political ploy, rather than an essential release of classified intelligence, according to Democrats. If so, it was therefore propaganda. The consensus of opinion was that it was geared to give a reason for the President to fire the Department of Justice personnel who were investigating possible Russian involvement in the 2016 election.

In early February of 2017, the front page of the official Vatican newspaper had a fake interview with Pope Francis. Reactionaries in the Vatican have given the liberal Pope a great deal of trouble. But rumors and lies are not new to the Vatican. Pope Paul VI, Pope John II and Pope Benedict XVI have all had false rumors foisted against them by foes on the other end of the sacred political spectrum. It seems that using the power of propaganda is as often the motivating force in church circles as it is in secular squares and plazas. Getting what we want is more important than ethical behavior—even in religions.

The alt-right is that far-right group that is associated with Islamophobia and anti-Semitism, right-wing populism, neo-reactionary movements, etc. The Ku Klux Klan would be a small part of this group. Neo-Nazis and some men's rights advocates (anti-feminists) could also be included, but there are far more individuals and splinter groups. Depending on the situation, they may or may not use violence.

Reactionary propagandists in Europe and America today are more likely to focus on immigrants who are racially identifiable and who profess a different religious belief. The Mexicans and Muslims in America have been major targets for President Donald Trump. Moroccans have been the major target of Geert Wilders in the Netherlands. The Brexit vote seemed to target most immigrants whether from the EU or from other countries.

Some of these reactionary groups are occasionally violent. But, as with all people, they may shift a bit along the spectrum depending on the issues involved.

The reactionary groups that use propaganda to influence the voters have been very visible in recent years. Donald Trump's promise that he could bring back coal mining and steel production and make it pay were totally unrealistic. However, such promises got him elected.

Once he was in office he did follow through on his promises of eliminating the climate change ideas of President Obama--and the rest of the world. He attempted to undo the healthcare act that Obama had sanctioned. He struck at the airfield that had been used to bomb helpless citizens with gas. All of these would be reactionary actions which were approved by his supporters.

While a person may get into office using propaganda, if he or she follows the promises made, it is a rational reactionary development.

Some rather comical attempts at reactionary propaganda were recorded it 2017.

Reactionary commentators, Ann Coulter and Rush Limbaugh, said that hurricane Irma would be a light rain and that the media were exaggerating the severity of the storm to increase the fears of climate change. They said that it was only to advance the liberal political agenda. Then a few days later, Limbaugh had to cancel his program because his home in Palm Beach, Florida was being severely lashed by the imaginary storm.

A few weeks earlier after Hurricane Harvey had hit Texas, Coulter tweeted that "I don't believe Hurricane Harvey is God's punishment for Houston electing a lesbian mayor. But that is a more credible theory than that it was caused by 'climate change'."

The pandemic corona virus was downplayed by Donald Trump when he said, "fake news media and their partner, the Democrat Party, is doing everything to inflame the coronavirus situation." Why should people be alarmed, there had only been 150,000 cases worldwide and only about 6,000 deaths up to that time? A month later there were 1,500,000 cases and more than 80,000 deaths.

Immature and narcissistic people, as well as most politicians, rationalize or lie when they are blamed for something—or when they expect to be blamed. Trump's initial reaction to the corona virus, two months after it had inundated Wuhan, China and a month after the severe northern Italy and Iranian outbreaks, was that it was only the flu.

Trump has tried to reduce funding for the CDC (Centers for Disease Control) but Congress has generally not allowed it. His proposed 2021 budget proposal slashed $693 million from the CDC, a 9% reduction. And this was made after the Wuhan virus had caused havoc in China. Lucky for us, that the Congress has not followed his proposals. In spite of this, it is generally considered by authorities that our health institutions at the national level are underfunded. Employment at the CDC has been reduced by about 600 people during Trump's tenure. He also eliminated the key White House staff that was involved in responding to pandemic outbreaks.

Trump continually blames Obama for his lack of preparedness for the coronavirus. Even though the virus was not discovered until three years after Obama had left office. It seems that Trump should have blamed George Washington, because he started all of this "president stuff!"

Immature or narcissistic presidents like to blame anybody but themselves. They, like most people, "pass the buck" to somebody else down the line. President Harry Truman was one of the few who could accept the blame. As you know, on his desk he had to sign "the buck stops here."

While Trump likes to reassure himself that America has the greatest healthcare system in the world, in truth, the World Health Organization rates it as the 37th best— the worst of any developed country. Although it is getting better. A few years ago it was rated as the 39th best health delivery system.

In spite of what the president has been saying, as of this writing in early April of 2020, the USA has had 14,000 deaths from its more than 400,0000 cases—25% of the world's cases. China had 3,300 deaths from its 82,000 cases and had stopped the outbreak. Was America's response really is good as our President tells us?

## THE REACTIONARIES—THE FAR RIGHT

Many whom we call conservatives are actually reactionaries. Here we will discuss briefly both rational and irrational, yet honestly held, views that are reactionary.

Every ethical, religious, and political view is based on either non-provable basic assumptions, on tradition, on observation, or on what we have heard or seen.

Let us briefly look at these sources of religions, ethical theories, and political views. Each of these is generally grounded in what we call "basic assumptions." Basic assumptions cannot be proved. When one assumes that there is a supreme being this is a basic assumption which is not provable. You may say that it says so in the Bible, the Koran, the Upanishads, or any other set of scriptures. For example, if a person says "I believe in God," because it says in the Bible that God exists. And who wrote the Bible? God did. So we have a circular argument that doesn't prove a supreme being.

In political theories, many begin with the assumption that people are either equal or unequal. Of course, in our physical bodies we are obviously not equal. But is there something deeper and more meaningful than the body? Do we have a soul or a life force? Here again we get into basic assumptions— assumptions that are non-provable.

Other beliefs may come from personal experience. My job was taken by a Polish immigrant who worked cheaper than me. (He may also have worked better than me!) But the fact is, I lost my job and I don't like it. I may also observe that people who have come to my country do not share the same values as I do. They may wear hijabs or burkas, yarmulkes or black broad brimmed hats shading their full beards, they may wear a colored turban and a beard.

Beyond their looks, they may not work as hard and they may want to collect welfare money without having contributed much. When this is true, the native taxpayers have a legitimate gripe. Of course, it is not always true. The Somalians in the US are said to be the highest achieving immigrants from sub-Saharan Africa. But in Norway they are found to be the lowest achieving group, often with large families who are given financial aid for every child born.

There are two terms that sound contradictory that are both conservative approaches to economics. "Neo-conservatism" and "neoliberalism" are different but still in the same area of the spectrum. Neo-conservatism is concerned with honoring and living the past through traditional religious morality and the traditional "might makes right" military approach to safety and security.

## NEOCONSERVATISM

Neo-conservatism looks to history to see that the strongest country survives. They also look to history for morality. And American morality, they think, stems from Israel. For this reason, they want to protect Israel as the founding religion of the Western world.

Morality is often black-and-white. It is found in the Bible or what people think is in the Bible, like abortion prevention and homophobia. Divorce is evil; so is gay marriage.

In military terms the United States should use its power to democratize the world. Certainly, communism should be fought and social welfare programs should be chastised. Also, Ronald Reagan's tough stance on communism brought the wall in East Berlin down. National security is paramount.

## NEOLIBERALISM

Neoliberalism is a different kind of conservative approach to economics. It espouses economic freedom. Reagan and Thatcher used this theory to try to reduce state interference in economics while deregulating and privatizing state businesses. This approach to libertarianism will accept aspects of the liberal welfare state when they are really needed.

## ILLUSTRATIONS OF POWER IN REACTIONARY GOVERNING

In 2017 Turkish President Erdogan won a referendum that gave him much more power in his pro-Muslim leadership. It undid many of the democratic reforms put into place by Ataturk many years before. He controlled the press so that potential challengers in the presidential elections had weakened voices in their "democratic" elections. Maduro in Venezuela attempted to do the same thing. Donald Trump can't silence the free press so he treats it sarcastically as "fake news," unless it sings his praises, as does Fox News.

## PREJUDICE CAN BE POSITIVE OR NEGATIVE, RATIONAL OR IRRATIONAL

Prejudice means pre-judging. I have a positive prejudice for Italian restaurants and negative prejudice against Japanese restaurants. But the worst meal I've ever had was in an Italian restaurant in London, and I've had some of my very best meals in Japanese restaurants in Kyoto. So my pre-judging has not always been right.

A number of years ago in France there was a positive prejudice for Blacks and a negative prejudice against Algerians, who are Caucasians. The Blacks were generally in business or were university students, and their ebony-like skin was so beautiful. Some Algerians, on the other hand, were more likely to be antisocial and criminal.

We generally think of prejudice in terms of racial or religious ideas. If an American were prejudiced against Colin Powell or Condoleezza Rice because they were Republicans or were Black, that would be a very irrational prejudice because both are extremely intelligent and have provided great services to the country. I would place them in the top 25 of all current Americans.

Racial prejudice can also be experienced within the race. Two of my good friends, from my coaching days in the ghetto of Los Angeles, are Black. One time they related how they were walking down the street in Beverly Hills and heard steps behind them. They turned and saw that there were two white guys, so they were relieved. They, too, were prejudiced against young Black men. One of those friends had two brothers who were members of the Bloods. The last time we coached together in Compton, he warned me about wearing either red or blue clothes. Wearing red could get you shot by a Crip, while wearing blue could get you shot by a Blood. So there is a rational prejudice for wearing neutral colors.

Naturally the ideal is to take everyone as an individual and judge him or her by their ethical standards. Martin Luther King reportedly said, "don't hate me until I have earned it." The reactionaries often hate or distrust those who are not like them. It is psychologically comforting to want to keep what you have. It didn't do King Louis XVI much good in the French Revolution. Muammar Gaddafi met a similar fate.

Prejudice against those who are different is not always directed downward toward immigrants of lower social classes. In Malaysia there is often prejudice against the higher social class Chinese and Indians. One area where this happens is in higher education where Malays are often given preference over higher achieving Chinese. This also happens in the US universities, where the higher grades of Chinese students are often disregarded so that other races or athletes can balance the ethnic makeup of the student bodies.

In California, no race or ethnic group has ever received negative irrational prejudice like the Chinese and Japanese. In the 1850s "hanging a Chinaman" was great sport for a Saturday night. During World War II the Japanese were interned in camps to separate them from the general population. Germans and Italians, with whom we were also at war, were not so separated. But these Asians have had the last laugh! The Chinese have risen in society and now have achieved at a higher level than any other group—about two and half times higher than the Caucasians. And Japanese have achieved at about twice the level of the Caucasians.

## BUT IT IS COMFORTABLE BEING A REACTIONARY

Because of our universal inferiority feelings, we must put people down in order to feel better. Inferior men must keep all women down. Non-educated people must find objects for their power drives to be nurtured. Consequently, anyone who is different can be looked down upon. Catholics can look down on Protestants because they do not have the true Christian religion. Protestants can look down on Catholics because they are not allowed to make up their own minds on theological issues. Of course, both can look down on Jews because they didn't come along with the new teachings of Jesus. They forget that Jesus was always a Jew and there is no evidence that he would have ever have approved of a new religion in his name. Muslims, have the latest revelation from God, so they are better than any others. In fact, if you don't believe as they do, you are an infidel—a nonbeliever. Then of course the Mormons have an even later revelation so that makes them even more knowledgeable.

And so the story goes: let's go back to an earlier time when "we" were the dominant people and didn't have all these other people bothering us.

But how far back should we go? 600 years ago the Native Americans owned the Western hemisphere. About 200 years ago California belonged to Mexico. 2,000 years ago Palestine belonged to the Romans and 4,000 years ago it belonged to the Canaanites, many of whose descendants now inhabit Lebanon. Just how far back should thinking reactionaries go?

Small parties in many countries want to move backward in time to the earlier periods when there were few or no immigrants. Geert Wilders in the Netherlands, Marine Le Pen in France, the Alternative for Germany Party, the Golden Dawn Party in Greece and the Future Party in Norway are illustrations of nationalistic reactionary parties that oppose immigration. Nearly every European country has such movements, which vary from 5% to 30% in approval rates. The populist movement toward national sovereignty and against immigrants and those of very different religious beliefs has had recent success in America and the UK.

American reactionaries want to eliminate the conservatively tailored medical insurance bill (Affordable Care Act or "Obama Care") that Obama had suggested, which was actually not a very liberal approach, compared to the existing approaches to single payer plans or socialized medicine in all other advanced countries. Eliminating the federal option that President Obama proposed moved the president's moderate proposal (moderate in that it followed the existing plans of all other advanced nations) to a conservative capitalistic plan that was designed to enrich health insurance companies and their stockholders—among whom were many of the Congressmen on the committees that changed the originally proposed, more socialized, Obama health plan.

Here are another couple of instances! In March of 2007 Poland's delegate to the EU Parliament said that women are not entitled to equal pay because they are shorter, weaker, and less intelligent than men. Two years earlier he was sanctioned for giving a Nazi salute in parliament. This type of behavior is, of course, completely irrational—and reactionary.

Reactionaries also are likely to hold religious views that may or may not reflect the current views of a religion. Recently over 10,000 Norwegian Lutherans left their church because the church had decided to allow homosexuals to marry. In the US some Catholics want to return to the Latin mass rather than hearing it in English.

In India, the leader of Upper Pradesh, Uttar Adityanath, is a 44-year-old Hindu priest. The 220 million people in his state generally agree with him. He was India's youngest member of parliament when he was elected at 25. Adityanath is a high priest and wants to undo many of the laws that have changed Hindu history in India. For example, he wants to ban cow slaughtering. He wants to erect a Hindu temple to the Lord Ram on the site where he believes that God was born. One problem is that the sacred site is now covered with a Muslim mosque. Among his other reactionary ideas are that women are weak and are liable to turn into demons when they take jobs traditionally given to men. He also wants to eliminate the threat of Muslims converting Hindu Girls to the Western faith.

Enough?

Not yet!

In many parts of the world, religion would be a reactionary sort of belief. But in America and in the developing countries, religion is a moderate belief. Religion certainly has tradition in its favor.

Abortion, as a method of birth control, is opposed by people who think that it is prohibited in their Bible, Actually, the Jewish tradition saw life as beginning at birth, not at conception. The Catholic view traditionally had had life starting 1 to 2 months after conception—until 1869 when Pope Pius IX decided that life starts at conception. Many Protestants seem to have picked up the idea that life begins at conception or at implantation. They seem to relish the idea that there is a sanctity of life that begins well before any biblical verse determines it. They condemn humans for stopping a pregnancy—but don't condemn God. And, as we have said, it is God who is responsible for the greatest number of miscarriages and spontaneous abortions, which by far outnumber human initiated abortions.

## CONSERVATIVES—THE RIGHT

The conservatives in America would be more likely to uphold the values of liberty over equality. They should support equality of opportunity in education and in employment. Sadly, they do not often do this. However, such ideas as age discrimination and racial or ethnic discrimination are now the law of the land and should be upheld by conservatives. These laws were passed by Congresses that were overwhelmingly Democratic and liberal.

However, because of America's deep tradition in the importance of religion and the freedom of religion, dating back from the earliest colonists, unprovable faith commonly is more important than provable facts. America trails most of the world in the percentages of people who do not believe in global warming—especially that it is human caused. America also leads the developed world with the number of people who believe in religion. The true conservatives in America are therefore overwhelmingly protective of religions, or at least give lip service to these beliefs.

Unhappily—faith is more important than facts. Look at Trump's policies—the fact of climate change is denied, but the minority religious idea of the unproven soul entering the unseen microscopic ovum is affirmed and protected by legislation and by the appointment of judges that know the truth of a political promise. Blind belief is generally protected by our laws. Faith in any religion is sacred—and the closer your faith is to mine, the more sacred it is.

Recently, in Europe, the right-wing parties have been pushing more for welfare. This is unusual in that right-wing parties tend to be for liberty and more traditionally conservative values. It may be that now in Europe, the values that we are used to, such as with the welfare state, are being touted by right-wing parties, such as: in Poland, Hungary and in the opposition parties of France's National Front and the Netherlands' Freedom Party. It may not be so strange in that in Europe welfare issues, like health and pensions, which were very liberal ideas originally-- are now so ingrained in the tradition that the conservative parties want to conserve them.

## MODERATES –THE MIDDLE

The moderates in America are often called liberal. The true moderate is willing to look at what is working in the world and work slowly and effectively to make it work in America. By many criteria, President Obama was really largely a moderate. But he had many liberal ideas, ideas which would be considered moderate in Europe.

Most of the Democratic contenders in the 2020 primaries were in this group.

## LIBERALS—THE LEFT

The liberals in America would be quite moderate, and even often conservative compared to European values. Liberals tend to move toward both equal rights (which are essential to liberty) and the actual equality of the citizens.

In the 2020 primaries Elizabeth Warren and Bernie Sanders were in this group. They differed in how to finance a more comprehensive welfare state. Elizabeth wanted heavier taxes on the wealthy, while Bernie wanted more government ownership of some businesses.

The slogan that "Black lives matter," illustrates a plea for universal equality. The fact that many of the blacks killed were breaking the law is often forgotten. But does the penalty fit the crime when someone is attempting to avoid arrest and is therefore killed? A question is how might laws be enforced if suspects are allowed to run away. Should there be less lethal weapons, like Tasers, that might be more often used? But Billy the Kid didn't use Tasers and America still is guided by the spirit of what they mistakenly believe happened in the Wild West! Thank goodness, we have television to give us a true picture of yesterday and today. But the various CSI series may not portray accurately what went on in your neighborhood this morning!

In America, the movements toward Social Security, Medicaid, and Medicare are all liberal movements. Affirmative action and universal free education are liberal ideas. The equality of opportunity is a goal of all liberals and moderates and many conservatives. It is frustrated by the fact that the Constitution gives the states the rights to education and the states allow for many local school districts to decide much of the curriculum—which is often far from the verifiable facts and aesthetic appreciations necessary for a real education. (See Revitalizing Democracy—the last sections of the book on education.)

Historically liberals have been for both equality and liberty, advocating for equal rights in freedom of speech, freedom of the press, freedom of religion, a democratic society, a secular government (separation of church and state), gender equality, and a cooperative globalization. Rights for homosexuals and transsexuals have recently been adopted. Once these values have found their way into society they are often adopted by the conservatives, so freedom of speech and of the press are accepted by most of those in the middle three categories of this spectrum. Those who don't want such freedoms for all, fall into the reactionary camp.

Absolute monarchy, a state religion, and the privileges of heredity are frowned upon by liberals. However. The hereditary privilege of inheritance may be accepted by liberals just as it is fundamental to the beliefs of reactionaries and conservatives. Liberals can be selfish, too!

## RADICALS—THE FAR LEFT

Franklin Roosevelt's liberal, if not radical, actions to pull the US out of the Great Depression through government funding of infrastructure, and the development of the beginnings of Social Security, put America on a welfare-state path. Then World War II brought it back effectively into the reactionary-capitalistic realm.

Radicals in our newer spectrum want faster change but are nonviolent. Martin Luther King in the US and Mohandas Gandhi in India would be examples of people who wanted progressive social change to happen faster. Much of the racial equality movement in America began in 1955 when Rosa Parks of Montgomery, Alabama refused to get up and give her bus seat to a white person. The second-class treatment of Blacks in the South angered them along with many whites. Rosa said that "I have learned over the years that when one's mind is made up, this diminishes fear; knowing what must be done does away the fear." It was that type of courage along with the non-violent resistance championed by King that changed the laws of the South—and the nation.

Many people, Black and white, were subjected to police maltreatment— cattle prods and dogs, as well as jail. Nine years after Rosa's heroic deed, The Civil Rights Act of 1964 was passed—and non-violence won the day.

## THE RADICAL PROPAGANDISTS—THE FAR-FAR LEFT

These people use propaganda, lies, fake news and other non-violent, non-rational methods to convert others to their ideas.

PETA, People for the Ethical Treatment of Animals, has a videogame in which the player can punch animal-experimenting scientists. They have publicized to children that their parents are evil because they feed them animals.

The umbrella revolution in Hong Kong in 2014 was a peaceful protest against China's heavy hand in ruling their recently acquired province.

Because the far right tends to be ruled by tradition, such as religion and laissez-faire capitalistic beliefs, it is often attacked by the liberals for being unscientific, in the case of religion and being unloving and unjust, in the case of capitalism. Consequently their "propaganda" is likely to be based on science and on humanitarian ethics.

Conservatives complain that media coverage has a liberal bias about such things as: the theory of evolution of humans; the existence of climate change, especially that caused by humans (such as Al Gore's "An Inconvenient Truth" promoting environmentalism), and the left's acceptance of non-traditional sexualities as shown in Disney's "Friends for Change", which shows homosexuals and transgender people as normal.

VIOLENT RADICAL ACTIONS—THE FAR-FAR-FAR LEFT

Among the most violent radical actions have been the American and French revolutions—fighting the over-controlling king in both cases, and the controlling Church in the case of the French.

Revolutions and uprisings have been recorded since early in Egyptian history. There have been hundreds, some were reactionary, others were radical— like the Cuban revolution in the late 1950s and the English Revolution in the mid-17th century. Lenin's revolution, and that of Mao, also qualify.

Antifa is a militant leftist organization that traces its roots to the 1920s and '30s, when militant leftists battled fascists in the streets of Germany, Italy, and Spain. It was involved in the violence in Charlottesville when it encountered the neo-Nazis. They popped up again in San Francisco and were both praised as being anti-racist and condemned as being thugs.

PETA has also done some violent actions to advance their cause. Buckets of blood or green paint have been thrown on people wearing fur coats. Although the official line is that they do not cause violence, members of the organization often get carried away with their mission and resort to violence. Similarly, ALF, the Animal Liberation Front, ostensibly nonviolent, has had a number of violent clashes with scientists and has destroyed laboratories.

While not physically violent, economic sanctions may also be seen here. The US-led United Nations sanctioning of Russia, Iran, and North Korea are examples. The sanctions in Iran were certainly effective in forcing Iran to stop its nuclear arms buildup. They haven't yet had an effect on Russia in stopping its incursions into Ukraine or Syria, and they first seemed to have made North Korea more belligerent— but after the summits, we will see.

A recent lone wolf example of this far-left violence is the 66-year-old white man who shot at Republican Congressmen in June of 2017 while they practiced for a charity baseball game near Washington D.C. He had approached them earlier and asked which ones were Republicans.

As a reactionary parent (sic) you may withhold a week's allowance rather than bruising your hand spanking your less than perfect child. Either action might fit in this category—as economic violence!

AND SO

Those who have the power and the money are already unequal. Typically, they want to share neither their power nor their cash. They want the freedom to keep what they have.

So, throughout our spectrum we have many conundrums:
- ➤ Should we have absolute equality for every person no matter how they choose to live (i.e. Equal pay for everyone whether or not they work),
- ➤ Only equal rights for every person (should that include free education to whatever level a person can profit intellectually?)

➢ The liberty to achieve based on one's intelligence and work ethic, or on one's inheritance,
➢ To the degree that liberty and equality are often in conflict, which should we choose?

And—elected officials always charge their new communities to work together in their acceptance speeches. Is it really possible to expect all the people to reject their political views and accept the ideas of the victor?

# PART II
## WHAT KIND OF POLITICAL AND ECONOMIC GOVERNMENT DO I WANT

We have several factors to consider:

➤ Where will my ideal government lie along the spectrum of reactionary to liberal.

➤ Where will my government lie along the liberty through equality of opportunity to equality continuum

➤ How much should the state provide welfare? (Total health care, primary and secondary education, university education, how much paid vacation, parental leave, adequate pensions at what age, shorter workweek, mental health care, disability concerns.

➤ Where should we be on the communism>socialism>capitalism>feudalism continuum?

➤ Where will the revenues for my government be raised? (Taxes, borrowing, devaluing currency, how much socialism?)

## SELFISH CAPITALISM OR LOVING SOCIALISM—DO WE REALLY UNDERSTAND THE OPTIONS?

Most people in the world are selfish. We want more than we will give. The loving people are willing to give more than they get. Have we thought our way to how we will vote or are we really just protecting our own selfish interests in spite of the fact that we will be better off if we expand our thinking?

Nearly 200 years ago de Tocqueville observed that "In the United States, the majority undertakes to supply a multitude of ready-made opinions for the use of individuals, who are thus relieved from the necessity of forming opinions of their own." (Book One, Chapter II.)

In America, so many of us are handicapped by the lack of knowledge about how other parts of the world work. We want China's vibrant economy, but we don't want their low wages, their autocracy, and their reduced freedom and rights. We want the happiness of the Scandinavian countries but are not willing to increase our taxes by 50% to have free medical care, free education through the PhD, greater pensions, shorter workweeks and more vacations. The Norwegians even give extra pay in December to buy presents, and extra pay in the summer for vacations.

## PROPAGANDA

In the U.S., taking money out of the wallets of the wealthy and using it for the welfare of the population has been minimized by decades of propaganda. Among the lies and innuendos of the propaganda are that:

> Socialism creates a "nanny state." And we certainly don't want to go back to the comfort mommy provided. Real men make their own way—and will step on anyone who gets in their way.

> The Soviets in the USSR tried socialism-- and the autocrats and their secret police took away peoples' rights. Stalin's reign of terror killed an estimated 20 million people. This has nothing to do with socialism, but everything to do with psychotic autocracy.

> This is true, but no Western state, using socialism today, follows any aspects of the Soviet system. In formal logic, this is called setting up a straw man, then knocking it down. It would be similar to saying that democracy is a terrible form of government because it was responsible for the death of Socrates.

The propagandists imply that people will be happier without socialism, but:

The UN Happiness Report has all of the socialist-welfare states far above the U.S., which is 19th. The 2019 survey measures income, life expectancy, individual freedom, generosity and perception of corruption. The top 20 ranking is:

1. Finland, 2. Denmark, 3. Norway, 4. Iceland, 5. Netherlands,
6. Switzerland, 7. Sweden, 8. New Zealand, 9 . Canada, 10. Austria,
11. Australia, 12. Costa Rica, 13. Israel, 14. Luxembourg, 15. United Kingdom

16. Ireland, 17. Germany, 18 Belgium, 19. USA, 20. Czech Republic

All of the countries ranked above the U.S. have more welfare state elements than does the U.S. If we look at the median income, the income on the exact middle of the population, we find that the US has the sixth highest median income, all five countries that have higher incomes are socialist-welfare states.

Additionally, Norway, Iceland and Sweden—all socialist-welfare states—have more billionaires per million people, than does America. In fact, the U.S. ranks 13th in the world in the number of billionaires per million people. How long are intelligent Americans going to buy the reactionary capitalist propaganda? Now that the American capitalist propaganda is dented, if not shattered, let's look a little deeper.

Don't these authoritative surveys make you feel all warm and cuddly about the blessings of capitalism? We might remember what Bob Marley sang, "Some people are so poor that all they have is money."

WELFARE STATE POSSIBILITIES

Among the programs that may be included in a welfare state program are: free medical care, free education from age one through the doctorate, parental leave from birth to over one year,  free prescription drugs, free transportation for elderly and disabled, paid vacation for at least one month, bonuses for the winter and summer holidays, paid sick leave, adequate and generous pensions, employment guaranteed, adequate public transportation, aid to businesses, mental health care, aid for sports and the arts, etc. Such services obviously require a great deal of money—40 to 50% of the GDP (gross domestic product of good and services sold/produced by a country). This income has to come from:

➢ Immediate taxes (individual and corporate—income and use-sales taxes),

➢ Delayed taxation by borrowing or devaluing currency,

➢ Government ownership of some of the means of production (socialism).

IMMEDIATE TAXING

People being selfish, do not like to pay taxes. They don't mind some tax on income and some tax on sales. But when they make a great deal of money, they don't want taxes on their wealth before or after they die. The rich often evade taxes by putting money in tax-free offshore accounts in any of sixty countries, including Panama, Cayman Islands, Bermuda and Samoa.

They also fight inheritance taxes, which they often call "death taxes," because it is only fair to give great sums of money to their children, who have not earned it. But where else should these silver-spooned cherubs get the money for their cocaine and caviar? And since Jefferson wrote that we are all created equal, taking the wealth of a corpse, through inheritance taxes, would be unpatriotic.

Income taxes can be graduated or the tax can be flat, with everyone paying the same percentage of their incomes. Rich individuals and corporations spend a great deal on lobbyists and accountants to be certain that there are enough deductions, tax credits, and loopholes to make certain that one's taxes are as low as possible.

Sixty major corporations paid no income taxes in 2018. Earlier this year, ITEP reported that Netflix and Amazon paid no federal income taxes. Other companies on this list include Chevron, Delta Airlines, Eli Lilly, General Motors, Gannett, Goodyear Tire and Rubber, Halliburton, IBM, JetBlue Airways, Principal Financial, Salesforce.com, US Steel, and Whirlpool. Amazon's gross profit was over $70 billion. Its net profit was only $11.5 billion. No wonder Jeff Bezos, the world's richest person, has to eat all his meals at McDonalds. After paying lobbyists $17 million to "bribe" lawmakers, there was little left to feed the government—or himself.

The capitalists control a large number of our representatives, many of whom are capitalists themselves. So, we must keep taxes low for all of our living citizens and corporations.

Not all countries tax the same. In Europe the income taxes and sales taxes are higher. The property taxes are much lower. Gasoline taxes are much higher.

Scandinavian countries are well-known for their broad social safety net and their public funding of services such as universal healthcare, higher education, parental leave, and child and elder care. High levels of public spending naturally require high levels of taxation. In 2018, Denmark's tax as a percent of GDP was at 44.9%, Norway's at 39.0%% and Sweden's at 43.9%. This compares to a ratio of 24.3% in the United States. But under Trump, 5% of the GDP was borrowed each year. So, the current American tax burden is 29.3%, part of the current debt to be paid by future generations! Very fair to let your children pay for what you wanted!

In Europe, generally speaking, sales taxes are about three times higher than in the U.S. Gasoline taxes about twice as high. Property taxes are much lower. Payroll taxes are higher, but so are the pensions.

Marginal corporate tax rates in Scandinavian countries are around the OECD average of 25% and much more competitive than the United States' previous rate. Denmark's corporate income tax rate is 24.5%, Norway's general corporate income tax rate is 27%, and Sweden has a corporate tax rate of 22 %. The U.S. marginal tax rate on corporations was much higher at 39.15% (average of federal and state) before Trump's tax cuts of 2017. He reduced it to 21%.

The taxation of capital income (capital gains and dividends) in Scandinavian countries is similar to the United States with the exception of Denmark. Denmark's tax rate on dividends and capital gains is close to the highest in the OECD at 42 percent. As an example of the revenue needed:

BUDGETS FOR 2018

| | USA | Norway | Sweden | Denmark |
|---|---|---|---|---|
| Budget in billion $ | 3,422 | 135 | 111 | 114 |
| Immediate taxes % of GDP | 24.3% | 39% | 43.9% | 44.9% |
| Delayed taxes (borrowing)` | 5% | | | |
| Transferred from Oil Fund | | 2.7% | | |

Sources of revenue by type of taxation:
Taxes collected as share of GDP (Gross Domestic Product)

| For 2018 | | USA | Norway | Sweden | Denmark |
|---|---|---|---|---|---|
| Individual taxes | 9.9% | 9.9 | 12.7 | 24.4 | |
| Payroll taxes | | 6.1 | 10.1 | 9.7 | included above |
| Property taxes | | 3.0 | 1.3 | 1.0 | 1.8 |
| Consumption (sales) | 4.3 | 11.7 | 12.3 | 14.7 | |
| Corporate taxes | 1.1 | 6.0 | 3.0 | 2.9 | |
| Other | | 0 | 0.1 | 5.3 | 1.0 |

PER CAPITA SHARE OF NATIONAL DEBT

Denmark $20.700
Sweden  $21,000

USA       $72,000
Norway none (Per capita share of oil fund is +$195,000)

## WHAT ARE COUNTRIES GETTING FROM THEIR TAXES

|  | USA | NORWAY | SWEDEN | DENMARK |
|---|---|---|---|---|
| University tuition |  |  |  |  |
| In state average | $10,200 | free | free | free |
| Out of state average | $26,000 |  |  |  |
| Parent leave paid | No | 12 months | 16mo. | 11.5 mo. |
| Per-child support |  |  |  |  |
| payments per year | 0 | $2600 | $3500 | $2800 |
|  | Some if poor |  |  |  |
| Health insurance |  |  |  |  |
| Premiums | $5200 | free | free | free |
| Out of pocket |  |  |  |  |
| Health-care costs | $6200 | $200 | $250 |  |

(All prescription drug costs are included in the figures above.)

(The World Health Organization's international ranking of health care systems lists:
Norway 11th, Sweden 23rd, Denmark 34th, USA 37th)

Health care will be discussed later in the book, however: insurance company CEO salaries and stockholder profits loom large, doctors' expenses for insurance clerks, lawyer fees for mal-practice cases, and prescription drug costs are among the major factors.

## DELAYED TAXATION BY BORROWING OR DEVALUING CURRENCY

Since American politicians must promise to reduce or limit taxation if they want to be elected, borrowing is the way to go. It's just like having a credit card. Just pay some yearly interest. And, most important, few taxpayers are aware of their increasing tax debt. Just look at what happened to Greece

America has the largest national debt in the world. All recent presidents have added to it.

Economists tell us to pay down the debt during good times, then borrow more during bad times. We owe over $17 trillion to individuals, investors and other nations and over $6 trillion to ourselves, primarily to our government pension funds like Social Security and the federal and military pension funds. We now owe $23.25 trillion in a good economy. Trump has added $3 trillion in three years and has signed into law a great deal more when the funds for his programs are needed.

Since promising tax cuts is the yellow brick road to elections, just borrow more to pay for more cuts. So hide the taxes from the taxpayers—then let their children pay the consequences! Most people are unaware that every trillion dollars borrowed adds a debt of $3030 to everyone's share of the national debt—now $71,212 for every person in the US, or $285,000 for a family of four. Because of the corona pandemic and the economic chaos, two trillion more was borrowed, so now it's over $25 trillion, about $75,000 per citizen or $200,000 per taxpayer, that is owed. But politicians need not worry, they will be retired or dead when the money is due.

When campaigning Trump promised to eliminate the national debt within eight years. Was this a lie told to get Republican votes? He actually increased it a trillion dollars a year each of his first three years. Then, because of COVID-19, he added another two trillion. Because of the healthy economy that he inherited from Obama, he should have paid down some of the debt the first three years, but the $2 trillion borrowed in 2020, was necessary to help the corona-sick economy.

Since U.S. treasury bills are supposedly as good as gold, many will lend to us. China and Japan have lent us over a trillion dollars each. The UK, well over $300 billion.

How about devaluing the dollar? There are now about 1.75 trillion dollars floating around the world. We could just print 24 trillion more dollars and pay off the whole debt. But then every dollar would only be worth 7 cents in today's money. So, a Mercedes sedan, a bottle of French wine, or a Samsung phone would cost 14 times more than they do now. And you'd never be able to travel outside of the 50 states.

An example of what might happen can be seen in Zimbabwe. In 1980 the government  introduced the Zimbabwean dollar which was equal to the American dollar. By 2007, due to inflation and corruption, $100 trillion Zimbabwean dollars could buy you a loaf of bread, but it wasn't enough for bus fare.

Perhaps closer to home is the Greek near-bankruptcy. Greece is considered to be the most corrupt country in Europe—just nosing out Italy. On an international ranking of perceived corruption, Denmark is considered the least corrupt country in the world. Italy is 51 countries down the list and Greece is 60$^{th}$. Like people the world over, Greeks don't like to pay taxes. It's probably genetic—but the human genome has yet to identify the "don't pay taxes" gene. The more you are expected to pay, the less you like it!

So, if you have money, you buy enough legislators to change the items that are taxed, or the percentage they are taxed. We see that in America with the capital gains tax where you pay only half as much in taxes for selling stocks or property than you would pay if you make your money your with muscle or brain power. Those with a concept of justice would probably reverse these pillars of capitalist taxation!

Here are a few of the corrupt practices that are common in Greece.

Many of you who travel have noticed this tax avoidance scam. You go into a restaurant that has a decal on the door that it will accept your credit card. You ask the waiter if they will accept your card, and he affirms it. Then, when you present your card to pay either the card machine isn't working or the bank won't accept it. This commonly happens to me in Greece and Italy, never in Germany or Scandinavia!

Then there is the continual seeking of bribes. You may even see pictures in Greek hospitals with doctors with their hands out. Pay attention if you want to be treated soon—and effectively. You find corruption from the lowest to the highest levels of society and government. Then there is the non-reporting of taxes due. There is little chance that you will be caught, and if you are, little chance of being punished.

So what happened? Their creditors got tough. Their national debt went from 146% of GDP in 2010 to 181% in 2018. Guaranteed pensions were cut. Hospital allocations were reduced 25% in 2010. Pharmaceutical companies wouldn't sell drugs to Greece. All taxes were raised. The 46% tax avoidance was policed and reduced. Retirement, which had been as early as 50 for some, was moved up to 67 for most.

As countries borrow more, their bond ratings are often downgraded, so borrowing costs more in higher interest rates. The U.S., because of its economy is rated at or near the top in its ability to repay. Its government bonds are in the second level of desirability with a rating of AA+. Germany, Sweden and Norway are among the countries with the most desirable bonds at AAA. Greece is way down the list with a BB rating, but it is coming up!  South Africa's are rated much lower.

. As an example, US borrowing costs about 1.5%, Greek borrowing about 2.5%, and South African borrowing a bit over 6%. South Africa's interest as a share of their national budget is 17%. In the U.S. it is 10.1% up from 6.2% in 2016.

While Greece had the largest debt, compared to its gross domestic product, many Western countries owe a good part of their yearly total national production. The US owes 107% of its GDP. A few others are: Canada 88%, Spain 96%, UK 86%, France 99%, and Japan 233%. Japan owes most its debt to itself. China at 55% and Mexico at 54% are much lower, and Russia owes less than half the percent as Mexico. Just give a country a credit card and they will soon be shopping on Fifth Avenue or Rodeo Drive!

The US also borrows money from itself--$2.9 trillion from the Social Security Fund, $934 billion from the Personnel Management Retirement Fund (federal employees), Military Retirement Fund $931 billion, and Medicare $307 billion. Then it pays the bills out of its yearly Federal budget, rather than from the appropriate funds, because there isn't much left in them. But never fear, because the government can cut your pension or your health care whenever it needs to!

You eventually get to a point like Greece and Portugal. How many years before the retirement age is raised to where it will pay for itself? This would be in the mid-70s for the US. In Japan it should be about 80 for women and 75 for men, because they lead the world in longevity. The Japanese government is now suggesting 70 as the retirement age. I haven't heard the Japanese complaining yet, but when Putin wanted to raise the retirement age in Russia, national demonstrations erupted. When Macron suggested it in France, national strikes ensued. In a democracy, we want what we want—even if there is no money to pay for it! How can there be a problem, just print more money!

Hasn't anybody heard about what happened in Greece when they didn't have enough money to pay for what eager politicians had promised—and delivered??
WHERE ELSE CAN WE FIND THE MONEY FOR WHAT WE WANT?

It is obvious that most advanced countries want the government to supply welfare benefits, such as free education to age 18, free university tuition, free health care, adequate pensions, more vacation time, free child care, aid for disabled, a sound economic infrastructure (ie. Roads, bridges, water supplies, power generation, telecommunications, etc.), possibly housing and financial aid for the poor, jobs for the unemployed. These would be possible concerns of a welfare state.

Commonly the capitalists' propaganda equates the welfare state with Soviet socialism, communism, autocracy, and the loss of freedom. Much of this was true in the Soviet Union, but quite the opposite is true in Scandinavia.

In the USSR, secret police enforced a nation-wide socialism that was not effective as an economic system. The government owned all of the means of production, as it would in a communist economic system. People were paid at different rates, doctors and teachers were paid more than farmers and factory workers. In the 1960s the government allowed farmers to raise food on their own property, after working all day on the collective farm, and sell their fruits and vegetables on the open market. The entrepreneurship allowed better and cheaper produce to find its way to the dinner tables. I remember buying fruit by the road side and joking with the women selling their wares that we were all 'capitaliskis." Big laughs!

Autocratic socialism or communism is certainly not the way to go! But modern democratic socialism, as we find in the Nordic countries is gaining in popularity.

## GOVERNMENT OWNERSHIP OF INDUSTRIES

We find government ownership of industries in many political and economic systems. Here is a graph indicating the percentage of the top ten companies in a country that the government owns.

Countries that own more than a 10% interest in the top ten companies in their nations.

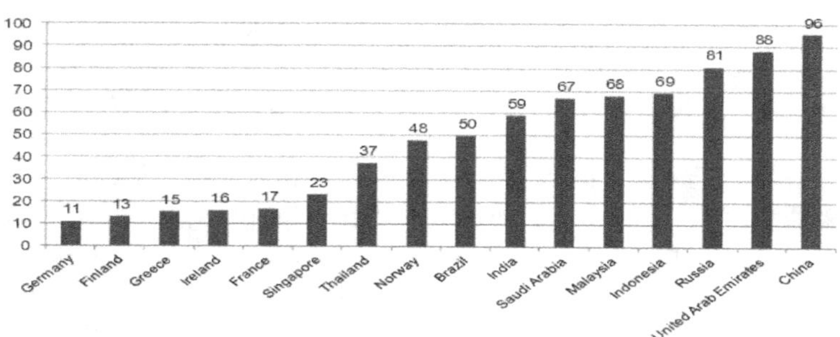


*Note*: Only countries with shares above 10% are shown.
*Source: Kowalski et al. (2013).*

These figures don't include typically owned state businesses, like utilities or the postal system. So, the above graph underestimates the true extent of governments' involvement in industry.

State ownership appears to dominate, but it is not restricted to, the emerging economies.

So, we might consider partial government ownership of industry to help finance the welfare state. That's real socialism. Based on China's socialistic economy run by its Communist party, we find that the government owns 96% of the shares in the top ten firms. The second place goes to the United Arab Emirates with 88% of the shares in the top ten companies. I didn't realize that the Emirates were a socialist federation. Of course, they are not!

Saudi Arabia, at number five, is certainly not investing for the population. The monarchy is the recipient of profits. So, the proceeds of state investing can go into the pocket of the capitalist monarch or be used for the citizens.

While these figures are clearly imposing, they should be seen as conservative for at least two reasons. First, our data does not include unlisted state-owned enterprises such as statutory enterprises in, for instance, postal services or utilities. Second, the state might also exert *de facto* control over a firm even while holding a minority share, for example, through a golden share or any other specific enabling legislation.

## SOCIALIST WELFARE STATE FINANCING—GOVERNMENT OWNING SOME OF THE MEANS OF PRODUCTION—FOR THE GOOD OF THE PEOPLE

Is the oil, under the ground owned by the people—who could pump it if owned by the government, or is it owned by the billionaires who stake a claim to it? Norway owns its oil.

♦ Are the air and the airways owned by the people or the billionaires-- who fly the airlines, own the telecoms, and utilize the internet? Many countries own their own airlines. Argentina owns the telecoms. The U.S. financed the Internet. Should it profit from its investment or just give it away?

♦ Should private industry profit from your illness or infirmity? Many countries own their hospitals. All advanced countries handle their own insurance—in fact, it isn't insurance, but a basic right paid from the country's general fund.

♦ NASA, funded by our taxpayers, has created about 2,000 spinoff technologies that businesses use and sell to us. Shouldn't the government be compensated for these, or take stocks in the companies that manufacture them—or manufacture them itself? Among them are: freeze-dried foods, memory foam for mattresses, battery operated tools and vacuum cleaners, computer technologies, infra-red ear thermometers, LASIK technology for ophthalmologists, artificial limb material, scratch resistant lenses, aircraft de-icing systems, enriched baby foods, and many hundreds more. But they are free to businesses in our capitalistic system.

♦ Since the government has some money—should it become a venture capitalist? What if the government had financed Microsoft, Google, IBM, Apple and VISA? Capitalists financed them, so they make the money! Why not the government?

♦ The government's bailout of industries due to the corona virus was a perfect time to take shares in some industries, like: airlines, hotels, cruise lines, and any other business that needed money. Venture capitalists who decided to help could take stocks, why not the government? The people who were responsible for paying off the national debt should get something for their generosity. United Airlines earned a net profit of several billion dollars in 2019, about $12 per share, but paid no income taxes. But the government gave them over $3 billion and lent them another $1.2 billion at low interest. . On the other side of the Atlantic, Norway would lend Norwegian Airlines only if it got matching loans from private lenders.

Cruise lines owned by Americans want American bail out funds. But Disney Cruises is registered under the Bahamian flag, Celebrity under the Liberian/Maltese flags, and Carnival under the flag of Panama--all to avoid US taxes and employment law. And most employees are from Asia, the Caribbean and East Europe. They are not in the bail-out package.

For the year 2018, Delta Airlines had a profit of over $5 billion. Its CEO had a total compensation package of nearly $14 million and a salary of nearly $900,000—and he's not even a Super Bowl quarterback! But Delta's carryover loses, depreciation, and other deductions gave it an income loss of $187 million, so it was in the minus 4% tax bracket. Their $3.3 million lobbying expenses, as part of the $104 million from the industry, helps to keep their taxes minimized or non-existent. However, they were quickly in line for benefits from the 2020 Federal subsistence package.

On March 22, 2020, Governor Andrew Cuomo of New York strongly suggested that when the government bales out companies it should charge interest or take shares in the companies because it is the taxpayers' money that is being used, so they should benefit from their generosity, not take a loss. Oh, my God! What is a socialist doing as the Governor of New York. Could it be that he is really, really smart?

We know in America, that communism and socialism are bad. We know that capitalism is the way that God intended economic systems to work. How else could the Vatican and the Mormon Church, or pastors like Joel Osteen, become so rich? Certainly "faith" is more important than "facts" in operating a government! Of course, in monasteries and convents they work on the communistic principle, "from each according to his abilities to each according to his needs." But what did God really want? In the early books of the Bible, it was the powerful people who succeeded. There was some chance for liberty, if you were in the family of the Pharaoh or the King. Warriors were also able to move up the social pecking order.

In the New Testament of the Christians, equality became more important and being poor is one of the greatest blessings-- because they will inherit the earth. While rich men will have as much trouble getting into heaven as a camel will have trying to maneuver through the eye of a needle. So how do Christian countries justify the acquisition of riches and the reality of the increasing number of poor and homeless people?

We justify all riches by capitalist propaganda and bribery. The democratically elected leaders of the American republic are often in the financial pockets of the capitalists. With the cost of about $1 million to be elected to the House of Representatives, and $6 million to be elected to the Senate, aspiring or sitting politicians must have money to gain or retain their seats. Lobbyist contributions buy them.

Honest politicians usually advocate government financed elections--as many countries have. But the capitalists would lose much of their control of the government. And they must be in control, or we will have socialism or communism. But what are we talking about when we say "socialism" or "communism?"

Capitalism is based on that basic need—selfishness. As babies, we are completely selfish. We cry when we are hungry, when we are uncomfortable, or when Aunt Minnie scares us. While not all capitalists are completely selfish, capitalism has always been based on making the capitalist the most money possible. But the selfish attitude permeates the capitalistic societies. Workers want more money. The citizens want better cars and bigger houses—and even more than one house! Politicians want more money and more power for themselves.

"I know of no country, indeed, where the love of money has taken stronger hold on the affections of men, and where the profounder contempt is expressed for the theory of the permanent equality of property." (Chapter III, Part I)

Recently, Governor Cuomo told the world that the makers of surgical masks, which were being sold for 85 cents six months before the corona virus hit—then when they were needed as medical necessities, the price was increased to $7. And ventilators were doubled in price.

If you are American, you may have noticed that when the corona virus hit, people invaded the markets and discount stores and hoarded food and toilet paper. Why? The toilet paper manufacturers hadn't gone out of business. But, "to hell with anyone else, I'm taking care of me!"

The Harvey Weinstein and Bill Cosby episodes show an often typical, "Me Tarzan-- Me want Jane" approach to the needs for sexual power. The "Me Too" movement has slowed this selfish approach to sexual power.

A recent series of studies done at Stanford University in the Psychology Department indicates that European Americans (meaning white) were better motivated to do things if they were told to "take charge" rather than being told it was for the common good, or that they should work together on a project. In fact, when the requirement to work together was enforced, it often decreased their motivation. Asian Americans, who had experienced both the American individualism and the Asian culture of interdependence, were found to be motivated by either approach. (January. Hamedani, Markus, and Fuln. "The Land of the Free, Interdependent Action Undermines Motivation." Psychological Science: Jan 2013)

And in the 1830s, Alexis de Tocqueville voiced his concern that the extreme individualism of the new American democracy could, if not curbed, could sap "the virtues of public life." We have looked at the happiest countries in the world, not here is a list of the happiest cities.

THE HAPPIEST CITIES IN THE WORLD

1. Helsinki, Finland, 2. Aarhus, Denmark, 3. Wellington, New Zealand, 4. Zurich, Switzerland, 5. Copenhagen, Denmark, 6. Bergen, Norway, 7. Oslo, Norway, 8. Tel Aviv, Israel, 9. Stockholm, Sweden, 10. Brisbane, Australia, 11. San Jose, Costa Rica,

12. Reykjavik, Iceland, 13. Toronto, Canada , 14. Melbourne, Australia, 15. Perth, Australia, 16. Auckland, New Zealand, 17. Christchurch, New Zealand, 18. Washington, USA, 19. Dallas, USA, 20. Sydney, Australia

Why are they happy? Most are in welfare state countries, and most are by the water. But wait a minute! Where are: Hollywood, New York City, San Francisco, Paris, London, Honolulu, and Beijing?

WHY ARE SOCIAL WELFARE NATIONS AND CITIES HAPPIER?

As we mentioned a few paragraphs ago, we start life as selfish little "critters." How come some people become unselfish? Why do some nations become "loving?" We need to look at the environments in which they were raised, the epigenetic effects on their genes, and possibly their genetics as well.

It clearly relates to people's capacities to love! But what is love? Is it psychological intimacy or just a warm feeling in your underwear? Can it be defined? When we say, "I love steak," or "I love my wife," or "I love my country," do we mean the same thing? There seems to be a great confusion in our society regarding a meaningful definition of love. We "make love" when we have sexual intercourse. We "fall in love" when we have an immediate, strong attraction to a particular person. We "love ice cream" because it tastes good; and often we equate love with sex-- and sex with lust.

Oh! Here we are back to semantics again!

Most people have some fuzzy idea of what human love is. This idea usually relates to some romantic notion developed from an exposure to the fantasies of fiction in literature and other expressive media. Psychologists have recently separated the real roots of love from the images romantic writers usually associated with the idea of love. It is, therefore, now possible to more precisely define love, it is also possible to see the essential relationships between real love and mental health.

It is often difficult, if not impossible, to comprehend an idea or an emotion if one has not experienced it. If one has not been loved as a small child, or has not been involved in a real love relationship, such as a mature husband-wife or parent-child relationship, it may be somewhat difficult to relate to the ideas developed in this chapter.

The idea of love can be based primarily on the knowledge of science, but it is tempered by insights and speculations of philosophers, religious thinkers, and poets. What will be examined is the definable, solid aspects of a love relationship and separate them from the romantic feelings which so often cloud our minds. Hopefully that most mis-used four letter word, <u>L-O-V-E</u>, can be defined ... or, at least, made clearer.

We must now look into the meaning of love as the psychological foundation of welfare states. I'm sure you have heard that the opposite of love is not hate—it is indifference. Welfare states are concerned with their citizens, reactionary capitalism is indifferent. So let us take a brief journey into the field of psychology to clarify what we mean by "love."


## WHAT IS LOVE?


Ashley Montague, writing for the <u>Encyclopedia of Mental Health,</u> has attempted to solve this enigma with his definition that:

"Love is the communication to another person of one's deep involvement in that person's welfare, of one's profound interest in him as a person, demonstrated by acts that support, stimulate, and contribute to the realization of that person's personality and its fulfillment."

With this definition in mind, he then echoes Freud's idea that, "Mental health is the ability to love and the ability to work." This is exactly what modern politicians are asking of their countries' citizens today. Most of our recent presidents have been very clear in their desire that people should take responsibility for their own lives and that they should work to improve the lives of others in their communities.

We can better understand what Montagu meant by breaking down the definition into its component parts:

"Love is the communication to another person." How <u>do</u> we communicate? If I say "I love you, baby." to a newly-born infant, the idea would vary according to the tone of my voice. If I coo it softly, the baby will receive a positive message; if I snarl it sharply, the baby will receive a negative message. So it is not only the actual words spoken that reveal the message, but also the tone of the voice used and one's body language.

There is evidence that non-verbal communication may account for as much as 90% of all communication. Communicating love non-verbally may be shown in hugging, pleasant facial expressions, various kinds of touching, or in actions which are not seen, but whose effects are experienced such as a father buying a book for his child. Even certain negative experiences, such as a child's spanking, may show a positive love effect to the child.

The person who "loves" must communicate a concern for, and an interest in, the persons he or she loves. And that communication should be in the form of actions that help the loved ones to achieve their fullest potentials. It is easier to illustrate loving actions from adults towards children than between adults--but that is also possible. Let's begin by looking at adults and some things they might do which are loving--or which appear to be loving but are not.

Adults often cannot actually love because their inferiority complexes and power drives get in the way. Real love between adults is shown where each person helps the other to be the best that he or she can be. It means helping them to fulfill worthwhile goals, helping them to eliminate harmful habits, saying things which make them feel good, and making them feel worthwhile. And welfare state attitudes tend to reinforce the idea that the society cares for you. This starts with the parental leave, where both mother and father take time with the newborn.

THE KINDS OF LOVE

There have been many words and meanings from other cultures that have been translated into the English word "love. "

*ROMANTIC LOVE* The words <u>eros</u> (Greek) and cupido (Latin) originally meant a sentimental attachment between people. "Love" can also mean desire (<u>libido</u> in Freudian terms). The gods of love, Eros and Cupid, were sources for these ideas of love. Our word, erotic, stems from Eros, and we all know about Cupid shooting his magic arrows to bind the hearts of passionate lovers. This is a personal experience, not a societal experience, so we won't venture up this avenue.

*BROTHERLY LOVE* is a second meaning of "love" comes from the Greek word "philia," which originally meant friendship or brotherly love. This is the type of love shown when people help others. Giving to a charity, assisting with a special group (such as Camp Fire Girls or Scouting), or just being a good neighbor, are examples of this type of love. Our word ''philanthropist'' comes from the root word *philia*. This is the type of love that welfare states propagate.

*ALTRUISTIC LOVE* The word "love" was also translated from the Greek word *agape,* seen as the highest form of love, utterly unselfish. It could be seen in the love of God for humanity or in the unselfish, sacrificing love of a person for others. Many of the Nobel Peace Prize winners exhibit this type of love. Albert Schweitzer or Mother Theresa are such examples. The welfare state might even exhibit this type of love, on occasion.

## WHERE DO WE LEARN TO LOVE?

Erich Fromm in his classic book, "The Art of Loving" on the importance of, and the ability to, love spent a good deal of time analyzing the kinds of love which people might show towards others. The kinds of love were differentiated according to: The qualifications of the persons who were to be the subjects of the loving actions (intelligence, sexual attraction, or simply the fact that they were human beings) and the relationship to the person doing the loving (such as a spouse or a child).

Fromm believed that in today's society people have become too far removed from the closeness and concern of earlier families—the extended family. This has resulted in a feeling of "aloneness" which can only be remedied by people becoming more concerned with each other. He said that learning to love is "the only satisfactory answer to the problem of human existence."

While Montagu defined the characteristics of concern and behavior necessary in <u>any</u> loving relationship, Fromm found some overlap and some differences depending on the type of relationship. So we might look to Fromm for another point of view and perhaps a broader perspective on the kinds of relationships in which loving behavior can occur.

The types of relationships in which Fromm found that love can exist include:

1.    Unconditional love, the ideal "mother love", in which the person is loved no matter what that person has done. This is also called "unconditional" love. Not all mothers exhibit this type of mother love. Many fathers do exhibit this unconditional love.

Some years ago there was a radio interview with a woman whose son was about to be executed for the slaying of two police officers. The mother kept repeating that, "her son was such a good boy. " She "loved" him in spite of what he had done. But one wonders how he would have turned out if she had really loved him early in life in the sense that Montagu describes in his definition.

2.    "Conditional love" is dependent on a condition in order for ''love'' to occur. In other words, the person is loved if that love has been earned somehow. It can be viewed as a kind of approval of a person because they have acted in a certain way. Sometimes parents "love" their children when they perform. The star quarterback is "loved"; the smart daughter is "loved. " Fromm associated this type of love with fathers, although he noted that many mothers also love ''conditionally.'' With this kind of ''love'' it is really ''What have you done for me lately'' that is the key. This really isn't love in the sense which Montagu defined.

3.    Spousal love is defined by Fromm as "evaluation and emotion. " It has been similarly and aptly described by the prominent European philosopher, Sophia Loren, as being "amorous reciprocal esteem. " Fromm and Loren are saying the same thing-- that loving a person of the opposite sex consists of liking the qualities of that person and being "turned on" by them in a sexual way.

4.	One can also "love" friends, a positive feeling for them and a willingness to help them if needed.

5.	One can love one's country. When President John Kennedy, said, "Ask not what your country can do for you, but ask what you can do for your country, " he was pointing out that people can feel and act for their country in a positive way. Immigrants often love their adopted country far more than the native-born citizens. The immigrants have standards by which to measure and can appreciate what their country has done for them. They may be more eager to help that country develop its potential.

6.	Love of humanity is the broadest application. This type of love is probably found most often in those who are religious. Jesus may be said to have been such a person; Albert Schweitzer in his ministry in Africa might be another; some missionaries might fall in this category. Many of those who served in the Peace Corps or the VISTA program might also qualify. Those who love their neighbors as themselves exemplify this type of love. This, as you can see, is basic to a welfare state.

Fromm has defined types of love based on the natures of the love objects and the attitude shown by the person who loves. In so doing, he has gone far afield of the Montagu definition which is concerned with the acts that a person does which develop another person's potential. Yet, Fromm's idea that "love is an unselfish attitude" and a psychological closeness (as Montagu identified it) permeates his work. Certainly his book <u>The Art of Loving</u> is a classic and should be read by anyone who wants a better understanding of this often nebulous idea of love.

Because of the various meanings of "love" brought to our language from other languages, it is understandable that we are confused about its meaning. But now, as modern psychologists have begun to understand the nature of love in the 20th century, they have been able to identify the essential elements that make up a "loving relationship." Do American politicians care? How many capitalists care?


## THE NEED FOR LOVE

If Erich Fromm is right, humans have a basic need for love. However, the needs that a person feels (such as the need to be popular or to be needed) may not indicate the basic needs in the person. People's basic needs (to be loved, to be able to love, to feel secure) may be overshadowed in their own minds by other needs that they feel (to make money, to be popular, to get married). We should keep in mind that it is our real needs, not those which we feel, which are essential in developing our mental health and happiness. How much would an ideal welfare state meet these needs?

### OVERCOMING OUR ALONENESS.

Albert Schweitzer, Nobel Peace Prize winner, said that "We are all so much together but we are all dying of aloneness." This is exactly Fromm's point. Fromm has continually emphasized that our greatest need in modern society is to overcome our aloneness. Modern economic necessities and the pursuit of wealth have separated us from the extended families which we had in earlier days--where people lived close to many relatives and friends. In those days there was more dependence on people. There was therefore a human warmth which surrounded most people. As people moved to the cities they often left the emotional coziness of the family and entered the emotional cold of a detached existence. The welfare state attempts to close this gap by putting people first.

In terms of love between people, Erich Fromm's "The Art of Loving" stressed the point that most people see love primarily as the problem of "being loved" rather than that of being the person who "does the loving." Then he emphasized that being able to love depends on one's capacity to love. This is something which we learn.

Erich Fromm was probably the first to point out how the capacity to love is developed, noting that while people believe that loving is natural and easy, the development of the capacity to love is actually a very difficult task. And when a person has learned to love, that person does not just love one other person, but rather he or she develops the generalized ability to love.

It is Fromm's thesis that we "learn to love by being loved." Love does not come naturally, it must be cultivated. Therefore, the best thing that parents can do for their children is to teach them how to love. This is done by example. Successfully ascending the staircase of learning how to love are the primary duties of parents, but the state can help. Looking at Fromm's ideas of how the ability to love develops, we can also see how the state may, and often does, aid in the process.

Fromm and many other prominent people studying the development of mentally-healthy people and healthy relationships, believe that self-respect should be developed in a child before its fourth or fifth year if it is to be an effective basis for the child's mental health and the ability to love.

Most welfare state countries give about a year off from work, with pay, with each parent allowed, or required, to take time bonding with the baby. This time is expected to be quality time in which the baby learns that it is important, thus gaining self-respect.

Self-love is the second stage in the development of the ability to love, according to Fromm. He makes it clear that self-love is not selfishness. Selfishness is seeing ourselves only—excluding other people, self-love is seeing ourselves in relation to other people. It can occur only if the person has developed self-respect. It is fundamental to a feeling of self-esteem.

Because of the relatively high cost of a welfare state, both parents generally work. This requires a kindergarten from about age one. With other children, and a pupil-teacher ratio of about five to one, the child has ample opportunity, and guidance, to play with others—and realize that they, too, are important.

Fromm notes that when a person "loves one's neighbor as one's self", it implies that the loving person's own uniqueness and integrity are respected. An understanding and appreciation of one's self is necessary before another person can be understood and appreciated. It is now much more often realized by psychologists that while love is often identified as a relationship with a particular person, it is essentially a matter of caring for oneself and others.

The generalized ability to love is the culmination of the development of love. When people feel real "self worth" and "self love", then their self-esteem and self-confidence make them sufficiently secure to be able to show this same attitude toward others. People who have developed this potential to love do not just love one or a few people, they love "generally. "

Dr. Leo Buscaglia, one of America's foremost advocates of "love", emphasized that "if you have love, you can give it.... It's a matter of sharing....I don't lose it because I still have it." If we are capable of loving we cannot be ambivalent to others. As we said earlier, the opposite of love is not hate--it is indifference. So a welfare-state society is a "loving" society.

With this generalized ability of love understood, it is easy to see how we can love more than one person at a time. In fact we may love many people at the same time. That is, we may do many things for these people to help them to be the best that they can be.

Ralph Waldo Emerson once wrote that, "Rings and jewels are not gifts, but apologies for gifts; the only true gift is a gift of oneself. " How often do we see the successful business executive working as many as seven days a week, playing golf with business associates during free time, seldom seeing his or her family. But he or she buys them off with gifts. Son gets a new car. Daughter is sent to the finest boarding school and the best summer camps. This person has put time into what he or she values -- the job. The money earned is then traded to ''buy off'' those whom are supposed to be loved. We can tell what people value by the amount of time they spend in various activities. But this is not the case with welfare states when they have the needed resources. They are there when you need them—but in addition to being there, they usually take the lead in caring. This caring attitude tends to permeate the society.

## WORKERS' RIGHTS

Workers, from the earliest days, have usually been little more than chattel. So they unionized. But the capitalists worked to increase the "right to work" laws that allowed people to work without being a union member. Judges and politicians, seldom having had experience of shoveling coal or working at a checkout counter, agreed with the capitalists in their quest for economic freedom, and "right to work" laws gave the freedom to capitalists to hire whom they wanted and the freedom to workers to not pay union dues--yet be covered by union negotiated pay raises and improved working conditions.

So the selfish, and short-sighted, worker did not have to pay union dues, but could profit from the union's negotiated pay raises. Consequently, U.S. union membership dropped nearly 50% from 1983 to today, from 20.1% to 10.3%. A good part of those were public sector workers, like teachers. Public sector workers are 33.6% unionized, compared to 6.2% of private sector workers. In Norway, 52% of workers are in unions. The U.S. percent of union workers is one of the lowest in the developed countries. So who is looking out for their interests?

As a result of the severe weakening of the unions, meaningful wage increases have not increased in 60 years. $2.50 in 1960 has equivalent purchasing power to $23 today, because of inflation. One factor is the increased cost of such things as health insurance provided by employers. The decline of unions and inadequate education are others.

But we have to look at the competition we didn't have in the 60s and 80s. Manufacturing labor costs per hour are: in China $6.50, in Mexico $4.90, and in Vietnam $3. In the U.S. it is $22.50. To compete, the U.S. workers would have to four to seven times faster or have more effective automation or more and better artificial intelligence, or offer different and better services. Things are different now!

But here is another factor to consider. The U.S. has the largest pay gap between CEOs and workers. In the U.S. it is 265 times more, in India 229 times more, in the UK 201 times more, in the Netherlands 171 times more, in Canada 149 times more, in Germany 136 times more, and in China 127 times more. By contrast in Norway the gap is only 16 times more.

The more socialistic welfare nations emphasize a more unselfish, equalitarian and loving approach to wages. The CEO of Equinor, the Norwegian state oil company earns $2.4 million, compared to Chevron's CEO at $19 million and the Netherlands Shell CEO at $24 million. Equinor earned $13.5 billion, Chevron $14.8 billion, and Shell $23.3 billion. So if we were to base CEO pay on pre-tax earnings, the Chevron CEO's salary would be about 10% more than the Equinor's CEO, or about $2.65 million, and Shell's CEO would earn about 60% more than Equinor's or $3.9 million.

Ahh! Capitalism! Lucky for the Equinor head, if his two million dollars won't buy his groceries for the year, he has the Norwegian welfare system to fall back on!

PRISON POPULATION

Norway has 60 per 100,000 imprisoned with 30% foreign-born, Sweden 61 per 100,000 and 20% foreign-born, Finland 53 per 100.000 and 17% foreign born, Denmark 71 imprisoned per 100/000 and 30% are foreign-born. By contrast, in the more capitalistic countries: USA has 655 imprisoned per 100,000 and 5.2% foreign born; England and Wales 140 per 100,000 imprisoned and 11% foreign-born, Canada 107 imprisoned per 100,000, foreign not reported.

Why might this be?

Since there is a straight-line graph clearly showing an exact correlation between the level of poverty and the level of imprisonment, perhaps the more equalitarian pay scales and the higher minimum wages are a factor. Another possibility might be that because of the availability of contraception and abortion, plus the state paid parental leave, the children will be more wanted and more attentively cared for.

Additionally, Norway has a 20% recidivism rate, while the US rate was 83% in one study for state prisoners, and 40% for non-violent and 64% for violent federal prisoners in another. This is probably due to the liberal idea of getting people ready to become gainful members of the society, while the more reactionary approach to imprisonment in America is to punish.

CHAPTER 8
WHERE SHOULD WE PLACE OUR INTERESTS?
IN OUR UNPROVEN BELIEFS OR IN OUR INTELLIGENCE AND
WHAT IS SHOWN TO BE EFFECTIVE

If we are to determine what is the best approach to a government, we must weigh the plusses and minuses of new programs, whether any existing programs should be pared down or eliminated, their costs, and increases in taxes. For example,

The U.S. pays $376 billion in interest on its $23 trillion in debt.
- ➢ Income taxes contribute $1.932 trillion or 50% of total receipts.
- ➢ Social Security, Medicare, and other payroll taxes add $1.373 trillion or 36%.
- ➢ Corporate taxes supply $284 billion or 7%.
- ➢ Excise taxes and tariffs contribute $141 billion or 4%.
- ➢ Earnings from the Federal Reserve's holdings add $71 billion or 2%. Those are interest payments on the U.S. Treasury debt the Fed acquired through quantitative easing.
- ➢ Estate taxes and other miscellaneous revenue supply the remaining 1%.

SPENDING

Prior to the corona virus pandemic the government expected to spend $4.829 trillion in 2021. Almost 60% of that pays for mandated benefits such as Social Security, Medicare, and Medicaid.

Discretionary spending would be $1.485 trillion. It pays for everything else.

Interest on the U.S. debt is estimated to be $378 billion. Interest on the approximate $23 trillion debt is the fastest-growing federal expense. It is expected to double by 2028. Currently, interest costs are only 0.13% to 1.35% depending on when the bond comes due—3 months to 30 years. These are historically low rates. They were almost 15% in 1980 and have averaged close to 5% in the last 70 years. If it were 5% interest today, the cost of interest would be $1.25 trillion, about 65% of the revenue from personal income taxes.

MANDATORY SPENDING

Mandatory spending is estimated at $2.966 trillion for 2021. This category includes entitlement programs such as Social Security, Medicare, and unemployment compensation. It also includes welfare programs such as Medicaid.

Social Security will be the biggest expense, budgeted at $1.151 trillion, Medicare at $722 billion and Medicaid at $448 billion.

Social Security costs are currently covered by payroll taxes and interest on investments. Until 2010, there was more coming into the Social Security Trust Fund than being paid out.

The Trust Fund's Board has estimated that the surplus will be depleted by 2034. Social Security revenue, from payroll taxes and interest earned, will then cover only 79% of the benefits promised to retirees.

Medicare is already underfunded because taxes withheld for the program don't pay for all benefits. Congress must use tax dollars to pay for a portion of it. Medicaid is 100% funded by the general fund.

The discretionary budget for 2021 is $1.485 trillion. It goes to the military ($646 billion), Homeland Security, Education, housing, disaster relief, etc.



The budget deficit is estimated at $966 billion. That's the difference between $3.863 trillion in revenue and $4.829 trillion in spending. This shortfall is added to the existing national debt.

Both the president and the Congress are responsible for the budget and any resulting debt.

## A LOOK AT POSSIBLE GOVERNMENT EMPHASES

Let us look for a minute at some possibilities that might be a part of governments based on different assumptions. We will look first at some of the possibilities that might be possible.

There are some elements of American government that would not be allowed in any intelligent democratic republic. Gerrymandering, while it can be seen as an exercise in liberty, since the people in power have the freedom to do what they want to preserve their power positions, unjustly interfere with the liberty of others to select their means of government. The U.S. Supreme Court, in 2019, allowed gerrymandering by a 5-4 decision, saying that it was a legislative decision in which judges should not be involved. This decision obviously thwarts the equal vote value of the citizens and eliminates the liberty of citizens to have their votes fairly counted.

The Electoral College is a similarly undemocratic obstacle to establishing a democratic republic. It was a well-thought-out mechanism for choosing a president in the 18$^{th}$ Century, but it has yielded minority presidents who were rated quite low after their presidencies.

Even the Supreme Court is often political, rather than judicial, because of the way it is chosen. Perhaps the members of the Federal judiciary should be selected by non-partisan judges, selecting judges that rule on the wording and intent of the Constitution.

The following possibilities for guidelines for governments would all accept the above three ideas if they were to choose democratic republics as their system of government.

## A GOVERNMENT BASED ON LIBERTY

There should be no restrictions to what any of us can do as long as they don't interfere with the liberty of others. People are not equal, so we should have total liberty to achieve what we want and to amuse ourselves as we would like. People are self-centered.

### Government

We might have a democratic republic or a king, but freedom is the basic value. "What I want is primary." We have minimal government because we don't want to be told what to do.

We have voting, but if people want to influence the voting with fake news and any other technique, they can do it.

We do have minimal policing because your freedom stops and my nose. If you punch me in the nose, I will complain about it. If a judge sentences you to prison, you must pay for your incarceration.

### Business

It is dog eat dog, and corruption is possible because we do not have restrictions on ethics in business. If you need to job, and you are qualified, you might be of the get one. If you plan to retire, you had better save more money or have retirement insurance because that will be your pension.

If you can get the job, great. If not, you starve. If you are worth it, you will be paid what you are worth, probably.

### Healthcare

It is up to you. If you want health insurance, it is available. If you don't have it, you suffer or die. No one will help you unless they are a friend or family that feels responsible. If there is a pandemic and the government tells you to stay inside in self-quarantine—do it only if you want to. Like one of the college students on Spring Break in Miami said in March of 2020, "I came here to party! If I get corona, that's the breaks!"

### Freedoms

You can say anything you want, see anything you want, and do anything you want as long as you do not hurt another person in your pursuits.

Hate speech is allowed, but you cannot punch or hurt another person, because they are also free, and you should respect that freedom.

Guns are available but you are not supposed to shoot people. That would interfere with their freedom. So if you shoot people or rape people, you will lose your freedom and can be killed.

Psycho-active drugs are free to use. If you become addicted, and nobody wants to take care of you, you die.

If you want to die, suicide is freely available. But you must pay any costs.

### Children

You can have as many children as you want, you can have an abortion, but you must pay for the education of your children-- at today's cost, it is about $10,000 per year up to age 18, then $25,000 a year through a university if you, or they, want a higher education.

### Religion

You can believe what you want, you can go to any religious ceremonies that you want, but the state will not allow religions any tax breaks. They will have to pay the same taxes as a business.

### A Comparison

A government emphasizing liberty may have happier people, but will probably not be as efficient. For example (as of April 9, 2020):

China had 57 cases per million population and 2 deaths per million (3,335 total deaths). Within 3 weeks of the first case it locked down the area infected, forcefully removed those with any symptoms, and kept people in their houses forcefully. Within 8 weeks it had pretty much shut down the disease—with only 50 to 60 new cases a day.

Norway had 1113 cases per million and 19 deaths per million (101 total deaths). It shut down the schools and many businesses, and required those with symptoms to quarantine themselves.

Sweden had 905 cases per million and 79 deaths per million (793 deaths total). It adopted the position to increase the cases and therefore increase the immunity. It kept its schools open. Businesses stayed open, When the death rate continued to rise, it recommended, but did not require, social distancing.

If Sweden's dead could talk, would they have preferred less liberty?

People may not be equal physically, but we all have equal souls. Not all theologians have believed this, but some do. So we should be treated equally. Besides that, society will work better and be more peaceful if we are treated equally. Of course, there will be those who do not pull their weight and there will be people who object to supporting lazy or inept people. Still, we will try to set up a society based on equality. It may not be exactly what Karl Marx assumed, but it is a possibility.

### The government

The government will have to be strong to force equality on an unequal population. It might be a single authoritarian or it might be an oligarchy or republic in which the authorities are committed to equalizing the society. What we see in the more democratic socialistic republics in the Scandinavian countries and in Oceania, there is more love-- more of an altruistic or unselfish attitude. But, of course, such an attitude does not happen overnight. It requires that parents and schools make this attitude primary.

We have jails for lawbreakers. But our attitude toward equality makes our punishments lighter and we are totally opposed to capital punishment. We emphasize rehabilitation in our prisons.

### Business

Because of our welfare state, more of our businesses are state owned. Naturally you will find some corruption because we cannot weed out all selfishness, because selfishness is a primitive attitude and need. We attempt to take care of the people, and hope that it will eliminate much of the selfish mentality.

Everyone shall have a job. Everyone should have adequate pay, but the pay will be based on knowledge and the work ethic. Everyone will have a pension based on the total income throughout one's life. The age of retirement will depend on and one's lifespan and the expected longevity of the person.

### Healthcare

The government provides total healthcare for all citizens including people visiting the country. This is paid for by taxes, both income and sales taxes.

### Freedoms

We allow no guns. We do allow suicide because we are equally entitled to determine our life course.

Drug abuse is handled by medical professionals who attempt to get people to understand why they have used drugs to escape our an unhappy reality. Those who inject drugs can get free needles and free drugs.

We allow freedom of speech regarding political questions. But we cannot allow hate speech. He also cannot allow pornography because it portrays some people as submissive to others, which is not equalitarian.

### Children

People can have children if they are capable of loving them and not abusing them. Eugenics is not even a consideration. All schooling is free through the university level.

### Religion

We support and allow religions that promote our equalitarian values.

## A GOVERNMENT THAT ESPOUSES EQUALITY OF OPPORTUNITY

For a government to be based on equality of opportunity, the opportunity must start much earlier. Children must be conceived that have the potential to compete and the basic psychological maturing and loving environments to be able to use their gifts in a way that will make them satisfied with their lives and to advance their society. So the equality of opportunity-based society will be based on passing on sperm and ova that have intellectual and physical potential but have eliminated as much as possible the negative genes such as the MAOA gene that is related to violence and other genes, such are related to hereditary diseases like: cystic fibrosis, Down syndrome, hemophilia, or sickle cell disease.

Not only are the genes important, but the epigenetic changes to genes that may have been passed on by recent ancestors. (Certain environmental stressors can "methylate" certain genes and cause them to not activate or cause other problems relating to the normal working of some genes.) They can also occur in the intrauterine environment, like the thalidomide damaged embryos of the 1950s and 1960s, in which severe physical deformities, cancers and heart problems are examples.

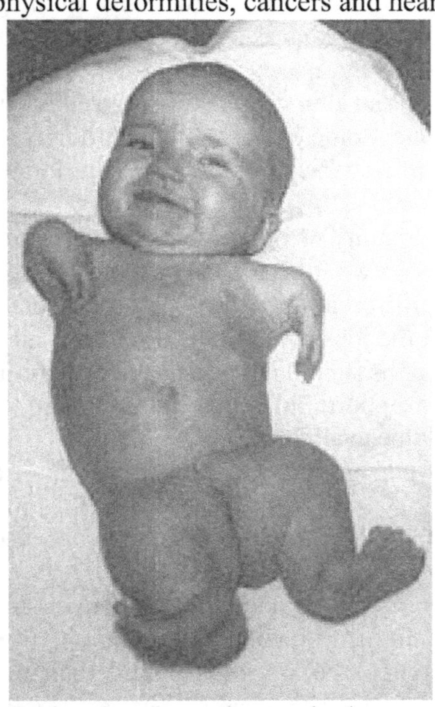

Schizophrenia, autism and other mental disorders are strongly associated with both genetic and epigenetic influences. Epigenetic examples are the maternal use of cocaine which is strongly associated with autism, and evidence of paternal use of cannabis is now indicating such a link.

Then after the baby is born, epigenetic changes will continue to be made. Some of these are positive, such as the effect of oxytocin, and some will be negative.

The SLC6A4 gene, on the 17$^{th}$ chromosome, aids in the working of the neurotransmitter serotonin. Serotonin in the brain is usually involved in calming feelings and the sense of well-being. Studies of females who had been physically, including sexually abused, from childhood and possibly including the teen-age years, often shows a methylation of the gene and a high risk of developing antisocial personality disorders. Other studies have shown similar results with males. This change in the gene's functioning was often accompanied by several brain structure changes, including more activation in the amygdala. Changes in the right amygdala could result in anxiety and aggression. One study of adolescents raised in lower socioeconomic situations showed higher methylation of this gene—possibly as a result of abusive environments.

If we were to advocate eugenics, some elements of the public would associate it with Hitler's idea of eugenics and therefore it would have a very negative connotation. Of course, Hitler loved his mother very much. In fact, he said that she was most important person in his life. So, should we also condemn all people who love their mothers?

It is a human failing that if we can find one character flaw, that should condemn the whole person. For example, Bill Cosby did much good in his life. His comedy shows made the nation laugh. His program, "The Cosby Show," was a great influence on racist America--that Blacks could be professional people. On the other hand, things that he did to obtain sex should have landed him in jail--and it did.

We overlook Thomas Jefferson's procreation with his slave Sally Hemings, and separate that, and his slave ownership, from his actions as a patriot and president, and his extension of America through the Louisiana Purchase.

Science clearly shows that our genetics and our epigenetics as well as our childhoods make us into the adults that we become. Some of us become murderers and spend our lives in prisons. Some of us become great leaders or otherwise contribute to the advancement of society.

The government in a society based on equality of opportunity would have to be strong enough to ensure that the children born would have every opportunity to succeed at very high levels. This would be quite different from the equalitarian society in which all were sitting as equal. We hope that the jobs available will be adequate to absorb the quality people that are produced. Pensions should not be a problem. Because of the quality of the people and the educational opportunities that are unlimited, the advantages of maximal health knowledge should be available.

Voting could be based on expertise. A person with greater knowledge of an issue could be given more votes.

Certainly, universal healthcare would be essential in a society based on equality of opportunity.

Free speech would be allowed in the areas of political thinking and philosophy. Hate speech would be disallowed because it would conflict with opportunity.

Drugs could be disallowed because people, who are free to make their lives better, should not resort to chemically satisfying their lives when real life satisfaction is preferable.

## NOT AS SIMPLE AS WE THOUGHT, EH?

No system of government can make everyone happy. Should we try to make the majority happier? The smartest? The richest (as we have now)? Those who think they are the holiest" Those that want chemically aroused pleasure? Those that want to conquer the world? Or who??

# CHAPTER 9

## LET'S THINK ABOUT IT

- Is happiness or low taxes more important?
- Is the physical health of the population or the economic health of the nation more important?
- To what degree do we want equality of opportunity?
- Are you ready to have the government elected with no outside funding? (The Supreme Court will not allow it because of the free speech Constitutional guarantee.)

If the Founding Fathers were around today, do you think that they would:

- Insist on an Electoral College?
- Insist on guaranteeing hate speech?
- Insist on allowing everyone to buy guns, especially assault rifles?
- Want free health care for all?
- Allow for the government borrowing to bail out companies from bankruptcies—especially if they did not pay taxes?
- Do we want to be told the truth?

## ARE WE FED UP WITH PROPAGANDA?

Should we make up our own minds on verifiable knowledge? The propaganda of the politicians and their capitalist captors have goy us into a peck of trouble with the borrowing that is invisible to most rapidly fashioning our concrete boots as our ship is sinking.

Here is a recent example of political propaganda that our President hoped we would believe, and if we listened to Fox News, we probably would.

## TRUMP'S CORONAVIRUS CLAIMS HAVEN'T MATCHED RESPONSE REALITY

In the winter of 2020, while other countries were giving expert advice on how to slow the spread of the corona virus, Trump used his bully pulpit to propagandize how the dangers were minimal and how his administration was prepared for it. This was another illustration of how the U.S. was behind most of the world.

- He said, "We were very prepared to handle the coronavirus outbreak." He also said, "There is an approved treatment, a vaccine coming soon." But the earliest would be 12 to 18 months.

- "There are plenty of protective masks in circulation." But hospitals had run out of masks.

- On January, 22 he said on a CNBC interview, "We have it totally under control. It's one person coming in from China. We have it under control. It's going to be just fine." In ten weeks the U.S. had 435,000 cases and 15,000 deaths.

- On January 30 in a speech in Michigan, he said, "We think we have it very well under control. We have very little problem in this country at this moment — five — and those people are all recuperating successfully. But we're working very closely with China and other countries, and we think it's going to have a very good ending for us … that I can assure you."

- On February 10 at the White House he said, "Now, the virus that we're talking about— you know, a lot of people think that goes away in April with the heat — as the heat comes in. Typically, that will go away in April. We're in great shape though. We have 12 cases — 11 cases, and many of them are in good shape now." By April there were nearly 400,000 active cases.

- February 23, speaking to reporters "We have it very much under control in this country."

- February 24, in a tweet "The Coronavirus is very much under control in the USA. We are in contact with everyone and all relevant countries. CDC & World Health have been working hard and very smart. Stock Market starting to look very good to me!"

- February 26: "And again, when you have 15 people, and the 15 within a couple of days is going to be down to close to zero, that's a pretty good job we've done." — Trump said at a press conference.

- February 26: "I think every aspect of our society should be prepared. I don't think it's going to come to that, especially with the fact that we're going down, not up. We're going very substantially down, not up." — Trump at a press conference, when asked if "U.S. schools should be preparing for a coronavirus spreading."

- February 27: "It's going to disappear. One day — it's like a miracle — it will disappear." — Trump at a White House meeting with African American leaders.

- February 29: "And I've gotten to know these professionals. They're incredible. And everything is under control. I mean, they're very, very cool. They've done it, and they've done it well. Everything is really under control." — Trump in a speech at the CPAC conference outside Washington, D.C.

- March 4: "[W]e have a very small number of people in this country [infected]. We have a big country. The biggest impact we had was when we took the 40-plus people [from a cruise ship]. ... We brought them back. We immediately quarantined them. But you add that to the numbers. But if you don't add that to the numbers, we're talking about very small numbers in the United States." — Trump at a White House meeting with airline CEOs.

- March 4: "Well, I think the 3.4% is really a false number." — Trump in an interview on Fox News, referring to the percentage of diagnosed COVID-19 patients worldwide who had died, as reported by the World Health Organization.

- March 7 when asked by a reporter whether he was concerned about the corona virus coming to Washington, D.C. Trump said, "No, I'm not concerned at all. No, we've done a great job with it." Within three weeks there were 650 cases and 12 deaths.

- March 9 Trump tweeted, "So last year 37,000 Americans died from the common Flu. Nothing is shut down, life & the economy go on. At this moment there are 546 confirmed cases of CoronaVirus, with 22 deaths. Think about that!" Within three weeks there were 6,100 deaths. COVID-19 is far more communicable than the flu.

- March17 he said, "I thought it was a pandemic long before it was called a pandemic."

Then on April 2, commenting on a model that predicted as many as a million dead if the pandemic was not handled properly in the U.S., he said, "I don't believe in those models, that's not what they are for."

While Trump has given overly optimistic timelines and overstated his accomplishments throughout his time in office, in the case of the coronavirus pandemic, his alternate version of events threatens to create unnecessary confusion among the public, potentially leading to a false sense of security, drawing criticism from public health experts and political opponents.

He said a decades-old malaria drug had been approved to treat COVID-19 and could be a "game changer." Moments later, the FDA said the drug was still going through the approval process to determine if it was safe and effective for coronavirus patients. In early April the CDC eliminated it as a possibility, based on studies just completed.

Trump's recent assurances about the scope of medical supplies on the way for health care workers also hasn't matched what has been available in the hospitals. "The masks are being made by the millions," Trump said on March 14. "Millions and millions. We have plenty now, but we're ordering for the millions. We're ordering worst-case scenario."

But a few days later, Trump had to call on the military to rush out protective supplies, as hospitals said they had to start reusing masks, making their own and asking the public for donations.

Trump said that the administration was not getting proper praise for the actions he had taken. "We haven't been given the credit we deserve," the president told reporters. "That I can tell you."

## DO WE REALLY WANT TO BE GOVERNED MORE EFFECTIVELY?

Getting what we want may be difficult. They may even require constitutional amendments. There is one such amendment that is only 6 states away from calling a constitutional convention. That would be for a balanced budget. Of course, in such a constitutional convention, other issues could be raised, like: eliminating non-political speech, such as hate speech, from the Supreme Court's rulings; eliminating the electoral college; bringing some sense into the right to own guns; and possibly requiring the federal government to own industries as a way of balancing the budget and increasing savings, while reducing the national debt. But such a change in American beliefs, when encountered by the industrialists and the controlling people in our two-party system.

The electoral college allows political parties to more easily manipulate the elections by concentrating on a few swing states. Controlling the spending by a balanced-budget amendment would remove that valuable ability to promise more but not showing it in today's taxes. Changing gun ownership rules would take away a major salve to sooth the very complexes of so many of our citizens. By having a gun, a macho tattoo, or a bull terrier-- people with inferiority complexes can show how powerful they really are!

Is it really important to have a government with any underlying values like equality? Should we stay with a government that allows certain amounts of freedom even when they may hurt society?

Is happiness even a worthwhile goal for a society? The Scandinavian countries think so, in fact, the European Union thinks so. But we don't want government entering into the private sector. Although it is expected when there is a major emergency, like a war or a pandemic.

As de Tocqueville observed, our traditions are deeply ingrained in us, so they must be right. So let us be content with our lowly place on the happiness index and remain content with our ranking as the worst healthcare system among the developed countries. Our extremely poor showings on our secondary school PISA testing shouldn't be a concern. We should continue to choose our teachers mainly from the lowest 20% of the college graduates, and let us continue to make our university education out of reach for superior, but poor, students.

**Why should I worry? I have my video games and my TV. What's to worry about?**

* 9 7 9 8 6 4 5 2 5 0 5 9 1 *